FabJob® Guide to

BECOME A WEDDING PLANNER

FOURTH EDITION

CATHERINE GOULET AND JAN RIDDELL

FABJOB® GUIDE TO
BECOME A WEDDING PLANNER
by Catherine Goulet and Jan Riddell

ISBN 1-894638-37-9

Fourth Edition

National Library of Canada Cataloguing in Publication Data

Goulet, Catherine, 1961-
FabJob guide to become a wedding planner / Catherine Goulet and Jan Riddell.

Includes bibliographical references.
ISBN 1-894638-37-9

1. Wedding supplies and services industry.   2. Weddings—Planning.   I. Riddell, Jan, 1953- II. Title.   III. Title: Guide to become a wedding planner.
HD9999.W372G68 2003   395.2'2   C2003-910991-7

Important Disclaimer: Although every effort has been made to ensure this guide is free from errors, this publication is sold with the understanding that the authors, editors, and publisher are not responsible for the results of any action taken on the basis of information in this work, nor for any errors or omissions. The publishers, and the authors and editors, expressly disclaim all and any liability to any person, whether a purchaser of this publication or not, in respect of anything and of the consequences of anything done or omitted to be done by any such person in reliance, whether whole or partial, upon the whole or any part of the contents of this publication. If expert advice is required, services of a competent professional person should be sought.

About the Websites Mentioned in this Guide: Although we aim to provide the information you need within the guide, we have also included a number of websites because readers have told us they appreciate knowing about sources of additional information. (**TIP:** Don't include a period at the end of a web address when you type it into your browser.) Due to the constant development of the Internet, websites can change. Any websites mentioned in this guide are included for the convenience of readers only. We are not responsible for the content of any sites except FabJob.com.

FabJob.com
19 Horizon View Court
Calgary, Alberta, Canada T3Z 3M5

FabJob.com
4603 NE University Village #224
Seattle, Washington, USA 98105

To order books in bulk, phone 403-949-2039
To arrange an author interview, phone 403-949-4980

www.FabJob.com

About the Authors

The *FabJob Guide to Become a Wedding Planner* was written by Catherine Goulet, Jan Riddell, and staff of FabJob.com, with insider advice provided by some of the world's leading wedding planners and associations. The contributors to this guide have planned hundreds of weddings of all kind.

 Catherine Goulet has planned weddings in the United States, England and Canada, and coordinated events in many other locations, including Africa, Australia, Bermuda, Barbados, the Channel Islands, Ireland, the Netherlands, and South America. Among the weddings she has attended are the wedding of Prince Edward to Sophie Rhys-Jones, and she coordinated an event in the Royal Enclosure at Royal Ascot (which is attended by the Queen of England and many other royals). Catherine is co-CEO of FabJob.com, a website named "the #1 place to get published online" by *Writer's Digest*, the world's most popular magazine for writers.

 **Jan Riddell** has planned and organized numerous weddings. In addition to planning and coordinating weddings, she has also catered weddings, and planned and coordinated a variety of other events, including dinners, dances, anniversary parties, and national and international events attracting thousands of people. As Project Manager for FabJob.com, Jan supervised the development of dozens of career guides. To assist you in having the career of your dreams, she brings her expertise in both wedding planning and career education to this guide.

Acknowledgements

Thank you to the many wedding planners and associations who have generously shared their knowledge in the creation of this guide. We personally wish to thank the following for their assistance and willingness to share their knowledge:

- Association of Bridal Consultants

- Robbi Ernst III, June Wedding, Inc.

- Nancy Freedman

- Maria Gracia

- Ann Nola, Association of Certified Professional Wedding Consultants

- Tricia Thomas, Wedding Careers Institute, Inc.

Opinions expressed in this guide are those of the authors and not necessarily those of individuals interviewed for the guide.

Contents

1. Introduction

1.1 Welcome to Wedding Planning

Congratulations on choosing a rewarding career as a wedding planner! You are joining a booming industry. It is estimated that 2.3 million weddings took place in the United States in 2004. According to the popular wedding website TheKnot.com, the average traditional wedding has nearly 200 guests and costs about $22,000. Planning a wedding that size (or almost any size!) takes a tremendous amount of time, effort and creativity.

Wedding planners will wear many different hats, including those of organizer, co-ordinator, supervisor, director and creator. As a wedding planner, you will ultimately be assisting your clients (the bride and the groom) with planning and creating a fabulous stress-free wedding experience to remember for the rest of their lives.

You will discover how to get started and succeed in this fabulous job in this guide, the *FabJob Guide to Become a Wedding Planner*.

This chapter lays the foundation for the rest of the guide. In the pages that follow, you will learn about the role of a wedding planner, discover the different titles used in this profession (bridal consultant, wedding planner, wedding co-ordinator, etc.), read about the many benefits of the career, and see the steps you will need to take to get started.

1.1.1 Wedding Planning as a Profession

Wedding planners have been around as long as people have been getting married, although, in the past, they often provided their services for free (with the exception of planners hired to work with celebrities and other wealthy people). In most cases, the unpaid wedding planners were friends or family of the bride. They were individuals with a natural ability for organizing a successful event, and were asked to help out without any expectation of being compensated for their time and assistance.

Wedding planning as a paid profession is relatively new. It is, however, a growing profession. With many couples living busy lives away from their immediate families, more brides and grooms are realizing the benefits of hiring someone to co-ordinate their wedding. Many couples now see the value that a wedding planner can bring them both in time and money saved, and in being able to experience a stress-free wedding day.

Catherine Goulet, a co-author of this guide, tells this story about her first experience with a wedding planner:

> A number of years ago, my husband and I were invited to a wedding out of town. The bride and groom both lived in the same city as we did, but had decided to get married in the city the bride had grown up in, a few hundred miles away.

> We arrived at the wedding location (a luxurious hotel overlooking the waterfront) the evening before the wedding, shortly before the rehearsal was to begin. We met up with the bride and groom and their numerous guests who had also arrived to participate in the festivities that night.

> The bride and groom looked radiant and relaxed without a hint of stress about them. This surprised me because I had been to so many weddings and seen how disorganized and stressed the bride and groom could be the evening before their wedding.

I also knew firsthand how much work was involved with planning a wedding, and how many last-minute details still needed to be handled right up until the wedding.

While I was contemplating the relaxed state of mind of the bride and groom, I noticed a woman walk in who graciously took control of the room, handed out itineraries and lined up all the participants to begin the rehearsal. Then it all made sense. This woman was a professional wedding planner who had been hired to organize, co-ordinate, direct and create a fabulous stress-free wedding experience for the bride and groom. The wedding planner worked magic as she handled all the last minute details and ensured that everyone knew the plan for the following day. I was impressed, and the bride and groom were happy and at ease.

After the wedding, I met up with the wedding planner and asked her about her fabulous job. She exuberantly told me that she had one of the most rewarding careers in the world. Not only did the wedding planner get to produce, co-ordinate and direct a special event (a wedding) but she also got to use her creative skills, her people skills and witness first hand the love between two people. Wow! That is what I call a "fab" job!

1.1.2 Benefits of This Career

As the story above illustrates, as a wedding planner you will enjoy a career with tremendous benefits. They include:

Rewarding Work

You will have an opportunity to do work that is fun and interesting. A career in wedding planning also offers plenty of variety. Chances are no two weddings you work on will be exactly the same, and each one will give you an opportunity to learn and grow.

Personal Fulfillment

Working as a wedding planner allows you to use your creativity and other talents. This career also allows you to see the results of your efforts, and have the satisfaction of making your vision a reality.

People

As a wedding planner you will meet and interact with a variety of people. You will support and assist the bride and groom, making their lives easier, and your work can help people to experience even more joy on a joyous occasion.

Growth Industry

The wedding business is a $50 billion a year industry. Faith Popcorn, an expert in consumer trends, noted back in 2000 that, "Time is the new money: people would rather spend money than time." This trend is still strong today. Rather than doing it themselves, more couples are hiring wedding planners to plan their special day.

Income

As a wedding planner, you can certainly earn a comfortable living. Many wedding planners charge their fees as a percentage (15-20%) of the total cost of the wedding. As the cost of weddings goes up, so does the wedding planner's potential income. Experienced wedding planners who work with wealthy clients may earn over $100,000 per year.

Freedom

If you start your own wedding planning business, you will enjoy the freedom of being your own boss. You can turn down work you don't want and take time off when you want to.

1.1.3 Job Titles

Wedding Planner is the most popular term to describe people in this profession (thanks to the 2001 movie *The Wedding Planner*, starring Jennifer Lopez, which brought this fabulous profession to the forefront).

However, there are actually a variety of titles used to describe people hired to plan weddings. You may hear any of these as you embark upon your new career, so it's good to be aware of them and understand what people may be referring to. Any of the following job titles may be used to refer to someone who plans weddings, although some of the terms may also have other meanings:

Bridal Consultant

Most bridal consultants are wedding planners who assist with all aspects of the wedding. This title is also used to refer to people who work in retail stores such as bridal shops, and specialize in working with brides.

Wedding Co-ordinator

The term "wedding co-ordinator" is sometimes used interchangeably with "wedding planner." However, some wedding co-ordinators are involved only in co-ordinating the wedding ceremony.

Wedding Consultant

The term "wedding consultant" refers to someone who owns a wedding planning business. A wedding consultant may plan the entire wedding, or simply give advice to couples who want to plan their own weddings.

Wedding Director

This expression is sometimes used in the southern U.S. for a wedding co-ordinator who is involved only with the wedding ceremony.

Wedding Planner

A wedding planner assists in planning and organizing any or all aspects of a wedding ceremony and reception. The next chapter of this guide covers the specific duties of a wedding planner.

While these titles may be used by people who have their own wedding planning businesses, they may also be used to describe people who work at part-time or full-time jobs in the wedding industry. For example, someone who works for a hotel or resort and spends most of their time booking facilities for weddings may be called a "wedding co-ordinator."

You may occasionally hear other titles such as "wedding specialist" or "wedding professional" used to describe people who are wedding planners or work in the wedding industry.

In this guide, except where noted, we use the term *wedding planner* to refer to any career that involves working with a bride and groom to help them arrange any aspect of their wedding ceremony and reception.

1.2 Inside This Guide

The *FabJob Guide to Become a Wedding Planner* is arranged to take you in a step-by-step manner through getting started and succeeding as a wedding planner. These steps, and the chapters they appear in, are as follows:

Chapter 2, *What a Wedding Planner Does*, explains the different services wedding planners provide and covers how to plan a wedding. In this chapter you will learn how to prepare a budget and time-line schedule, find helpful checklists, and learn how to plan a ceremony and wedding reception. You will also find valuable advice on working with vendors — companies that supply the products and services you will need to co-ordinate for the wedding.

Once you know what the job involves, chapter 3 will give you helpful information on *Developing Your Skills* so you can succeed in this career. You will find resources for enhancing your interpersonal skills, organizational ability, and creativity. This chapter also covers the best resources for learning wedding planning, and explains how to get experience.

Chapter 4 focuses on *Wedding Industry Jobs*. You will discover who hires wedding planners, bridal consultants and wedding co-ordinators, how to find out about job openings, how to prepare an effective resume and cover letter, and how to do well in an interview. You will even discover how to create your own job!

If you would like to *Start Your Own Business*, you will find good advice in chapter 5. Here you will find practical information such as the best resources for setting up your business. You will also learn vital information such as how to set your fees, how to market your services and attract clients, and how to do a client consultation. Finally, you will discover organizations that can certify you as a professional wedding planner.

When you're finished with this guide you will know what step to take next and where to go from there. By applying what you learn here, it's just a matter of time before you'll be where you want to be… in an exciting career as a Wedding Planner!

2. What a Wedding Planner Does

2.1 Services Provided by a Wedding Planner

Wedding planners can provide a variety of services, including:

- Complete planning and co-ordination of a wedding

- Partial planning of a wedding

- Rehearsal and wedding day services only

Some couples want a professional wedding planner to co-ordinate the entire wedding, while others want to plan parts of the wedding themselves and hire a wedding planner for the other parts (for example, to deal with vendors such as photographers, caterers, florists, etc.).

Other couples will decide to plan the entire wedding themselves; however, they understand the value of having someone supervise and direct everyone at the rehearsal and on the wedding day itself, and will hire a wedding planner for this role. Following is a more comprehensive breakdown of the various services that a wedding planner can provide.

2.1.1 Complete Wedding Planning Services

As mentioned above, some couples choose to put the complete planning and co-ordination of their wedding, from start to finish, in the hands of a professional wedding planner. The typical services you could provide for a "Complete Wedding Package" are as follows (more detail is provided in the next section of the guide):

- Initial consultation with the bride and groom

- Ongoing consultation and advice (e.g. on wedding etiquette) as required

- Preparing a budget

- Preparing a schedule/timeline and checklists

- Assisting with selection and booking of ceremony and reception venues

- Assisting with selecting and booking an officiant for the wedding

- Assisting with selecting a color scheme, theme and style of the wedding

- Assisting with the design, printing and mailing out of the invitations

- Tracking RSVPs and who will be attending

- Assisting with selection of wedding attire and accessories

- Finding, negotiating with and booking suitable vendors (e.g. baker, caterer, florist, photographer, printer, videographer, musicians, etc.)

- Reviewing vendors' contracts and co-ordinating with vendors

- Providing information to obtain a marriage license

- Ceremony planning

- Preparing itineraries, seating list, name plates

- Attending and overseeing the rehearsal (up to two hours)

- Instructing attendants about their duties

- Directing the processionals, recessionals and receiving line

- Reception planning

- Co-ordinating the collection of gifts received on the wedding day

- Wedding day co-ordination (up to 10 hours)

- Providing a stress-free day for the bride and groom

Additional services you could provide on top of the "Complete Wedding Package" for an additional fee are as follows. (Fees are covered in section 5.4.1 of this guide.)

- Announcing the engagement in the newspaper and/or sending out announcements

- Co-ordinating an engagement party

- Assisting with booking accommodations for out-of-town guests

- Preparing a unique ceremony and vows

- Assisting with planning the wedding shower and/or a get-together for the groomsmen

- Purchasing gifts for the bridal party

- Planning a rehearsal dinner/party

- Honeymoon planning

- Sending out thank-you cards

- Assisting with change-of-address paperwork

2.1.2 Partial Wedding Planning Services

Some couples want to plan their own weddings, but don't have time to do comparison shopping to check out all of the services and prices of the various vendors they will require for their wedding.

A wedding planner can save these couples a lot of valuable time and money by providing a short list of vendors who offer good service at reasonable prices. Additionally, a wedding planner who has been in the business for a while has likely developed good working relationships with many of the vendors and can ensure reliability.

Following is a listing of partial wedding planning services you can provide to your clients:

- Consultation with bride and groom

- Selecting suitable vendors such as:

  - Baker

  - Calligrapher

  - Caterer

  - Decorators

  - Florist

  - Musicians (soloist, organist, band, DJ, etc.)

  - Photographer

  - Printer (to print invitations, RSVP and thank-you cards, itineraries, etc.)

  - Rental facilities

  - Transportation providers

  - Videographer

  - Wedding attire providers (e.g. bridal shops)

- Negotiating with vendors

- Reviewing vendors' contracts

- Scheduling appointments with vendors for clients to meet with them (where necessary)

- Co-ordinating with vendors to ensure services/products are provided in a timely manner

- Co-ordinating final payment of vendors (if requested by client)

- Ongoing updates and consultation with clients about vendors' services/products

In addition to the above, the clients may also wish to have you provide (at an additional fee) the services of rehearsal and wedding day co-ordinator (see details below).

2.1.3 Rehearsal and Wedding Day Services Only

Some couples prefer to plan the majority of their wedding; however, they may wish to have an outside professional direct everyone at the rehearsal and oversee everything on the wedding day to ensure that everything runs smoothly.

If you are hired to provide rehearsal and wedding day services only, following are some of the services you could provide:

- Consultation with bride and groom to find out information about their wedding and determine how they wish the wedding to flow

- Preparation of a rehearsal and wedding day itinerary

- Attendance and direction at the rehearsal (up to two hours)

- Checking with vendors to confirm arrangements for the wedding day

- Attending, overseeing, and directing the ceremony and reception (up to 10 hours)

2.2 Preliminary Steps to Plan a Wedding

This section of the guide will provide you with step-by-step instructions and refer you to additional resources so that you can successfully plan a wedding from beginning to end.

2.2.1 Consultation with the Bride and Groom

The first thing you will need to do is meet with the bride and the groom and find out exactly what type of wedding they want and what they envision their perfect wedding to look like.

You can begin by getting to know about your new clients by asking the couple some questions about themselves, including how they met, where they were when they got engaged, etc. Then you can start finding out what they envision for their perfect wedding day. Get them to imagine what their ideal wedding would look like and ask them to communicate that to you.

The key to planning a dream wedding for your clients is to really listen to them to find out what will make their wedding day a perfect day for them, and to ask them clarifying questions if you are not sure about something. Find out about their likes and dislikes with respect to weddings they have been to in the past. This consultation is an ideal time to find out the couple's preferences about the following.

Style of Wedding

Do the bride and groom want a wedding that is formal or informal? They may prefer:

A traditional wedding

A wedding that is held at a place of worship such as a church or synagogue with a traditional ceremony that is officiated by a minister, rabbi or other clergymember. There are several bridal attendants, formal attire and traditional music.

A non-traditional wedding

A non-traditional wedding could be held anywhere from a park to a beach to the top of a mountain, or wherever their imagination will take them.

The officiant could be a Justice of the Peace (possibly a friend or even a relative). The wedding could have a fun theme to it such as a beach party or a western theme, etc. The ceremony could have unique vows written by the couple and the music could be performed by a talented friend.

Number of Guests

Determine approximately how many people they wish to have attend both the ceremony and the reception.

At this time, you can give your clients a *Guest List Form* (see the sample on page 22) and ask them to take it home to fill it out.

Mention to your clients that the more people who attend, the more costly the wedding will be and that this is something that should be taken into consideration while they are preparing their guest list.

Date and Time

Determine the date and time the couple wish to get married. If they are set on using a particular venue, determine any alternative date(s) and time(s) in case it is not available at their preferred time.

Money and Priorities

Find out how much money the couple have budgeted for their total wedding costs (excluding the honeymoon). You may find that your clients are on a shoestring budget but wish to have a glamorous fairytale wedding.

You will need to discuss with your clients the importance of being realistic and setting priorities. For example, is a fancy expensive location more important than the number of guests they can invite?

Guest List Form

Take the time to think about who you would like to invite to share in your special day. One thing to take into consideration is that a number of your guests will have a partner who they will bring, and this will count for two people. Also remember that the more guests you invite, the more costly your wedding will be.

You can start by making two separate lists: List No. 1 is "Really Want to Attend/Must Invite"; and List No. 2 is "Would be Nice to Invite." It is a good idea for us to send out the invitations early to those on List No. 1. If individuals on List No. 1 are not available to attend, then we can send out invitations to guests on List No. 2 in a timely manner. Please fill out all the information up to and including "Total No. Invited."

Name of Guest: _____

Name of Partner: _____

Address of Guest: _____

_____

Phone Number: _____

E-mail: _____

Total No. Invited: _____

Date Invite Mailed: _____

RSVP Received: _____

Total Attending Reception: _____

Name of Guest: _____

Name of Partner: _____

Address of Guest: _____

_____

Phone Number: _____

E-mail: _____

Total No. Invited: _____

Date Invite Mailed: _____

RSVP Received: _____

Total Attending Reception: _____

Likewise, find out what is absolutely essential and what they can do without. For instance, can they live with having a DJ instead of a live band at the reception?

It is important for your clients to determine their priorities so that you can prepare a realistic budget for them. (Budgeting is covered in the next section of the guide.)

Wedding Details

After you have discussed some of the main points about the wedding, get the bride and groom to complete a *Wedding Planning Registration Form* (you can create your own or use the sample on pages 24-28) so that you can find out more details to assist you with co-ordinating their wedding.

Your Role

Determine exactly what services the bride and groom want you to handle, and discuss your fees and contract with them. (Section 5.4 of this guide explains how to set your fees, and includes a sample contract for wedding planning services.)

2.2.2 Preparing a Budget

Not many brides and grooms are going to have an unlimited amount of funds for a fairytale wedding like that of Trista Rehn (TV's *The Bachelorette*) and Ryan Sutter, a $3.7 million extravaganza paid for by ABC, the broadcast company that aired the show.

Chances are, most of your clients will have a limited amount of funds they can spend on their wedding, which will make it necessary to prepare a wedding budget to work from.

> **TIP:** As mentioned in the introduction, the average traditional wedding in the U.S. costs about $22,000. Approximately 50% of the cost is the reception (food and drinks).

Sample Wedding Planning Registration Form

Contact Information:

Bride
Full name: _____
Home phone: _____
Work phone: _____
E-mail: _____
Fax: _____
Mailing address: _____
_____
_____
_____

Groom
Full name: _____
Home phone: _____
Work phone: _____
E-mail: _____
Fax: _____
Mailing address: _____
_____
_____
_____

Maid of Honor
Full name: _____
Home phone: _____

Best Man
Full name: _____
Home phone: _____

Other Information
Total number of bridesmaids: _____
Total number of groomsmen: _____

About the Wedding:

Style of Wedding

What style of wedding do you want (for example: traditional, simple, unique) and how do you envision your wedding day to look?

_____

_____

_____

_____

_____

_____

_____

Budget

Budgeted amount to work with: $_____

Ceremony

Proposed wedding date: _____
Desired wedding ceremony venue: _____
Time of day you wish to get married: _____
Number of people to attend ceremony: _____
Religion (if applicable):   _____
Officiant (e.g. Minister, J.P., etc.):   _____
Wedding color scheme: _____
Wedding theme (if applicable):   _____
Music you wish played at ceremony: _____
Desired decorations for ceremony: _____

Are there any religious or family customs that you wish to include within your ceremony?

_____

_____

_____

_____

Do you wish to include any special vows within your ceremony or any special exchanges (for example, the lighting of a unity candle)?

_____

_____

_____

_____

_____

Reception

Desired reception venue: _____

Time of day the reception is to start: _____

Number of people attending: _____

Please list any food preferences below:

_____

_____

_____

_____

_____

Please list any beverage preferences below:

_____

_____

_____

_____

_____

Please list any music preferences below:

_____

_____

_____

_____

_____

Wedding Planning Services

Please check off the items you would like our wedding planning company to coordinate for you or with you. If you prefer a particular vendor for any of the items that you would like co-ordinated below, please provide their name and phone number.

Please note that all of the items listed below are included with the "Complete Wedding Package" unless the item appears in italicized type. If you would like any of the extra items to be co-ordinated, there will be an extra fee (to be agreed upon.)

Service Desired	Preferred Vendor
❑ Announcement of engagement in newspaper	_____
❑ Engagement party	_____
❑ Design and/or mailing of invitations	_____
❑ Calligrapher	_____
❑ Printer	_____
❑ Tracking of guests attending	_____
❑ Wedding gown and accessories	_____
❑ Bridesmaids' attire and accessories	_____
❑ Appointment with hairstylist and/or makeup artist	_____
❑ Groomsmen's attire	_____
❑ Musician for ceremony	_____
❑ Flowers	_____
❑ Photographer	_____
❑ Videographer	_____

- ❏ Transportation   _____
- ❏ Decorations   _____
- ❏ Visitor's guest book   _____
- ❏ Caterer   _____
- ❏ Wedding cake   _____
- ❏ Table centerpieces   _____
- ❏ Wedding favors   _____
- ❏ Rental of tent, equipment, etc.   _____
  (if required)
- ❏ DJ, band or musicians for reception   _____
- ❏ Accommodation for out-of-town guests   _____
- ❏ Rehearsal dinner   _____
- ❏ Marriage license   _____
- ❏ Reception seating   _____
- ❏ Gift registry   _____
- ❏ Collection of gifts   _____
- ❏ Information on wedding etiquette   _____
- ❏ Announcement of wedding in   _____
  the newspaper
- ❏ Thank-you cards prepared and   _____
  sent out
- ❏ Gifts for the bridal party/groomsmen   _____
  and others
- ❏ Honeymoon planning   _____
- ❏ Information on passports, visas   _____
  and inoculations

After you have met with the bride and groom and know how many guests they wish to invite, what their priorities are, and how much money they have to work with, you can then start preparing a budget.

Budget Planners

To get you started, you can try some interactive budget planners online. **WeddingChannel.com** has an amazing budget calculator. You enter the total amount budgeted, the number of people invited and the total number of attendants. The budget calculator then determines the amount to spend on each item from the bridal attire to catering and everything else in between. The amounts can be adjusted based on the priorities of the bride and groom. (Note: In order to use the calculator, you will need to complete a short – and free – registration process).

Another interactive budget planner and a variety of budgeting tips can be found at the Bliss! Weddings site at **www.blissezine.com**. You may be able to find other budget planners with an online search.

After you have come up with an initial budget for your clients, you can track all budgeted amounts on the sample *Wedding Budget Form* which starts on the next page. This form can act as a checklist and it will give you something to work with to not only keep track of the amounts budgeted but also the amounts actually spent on each item.

Sample Wedding Budget Form

	Estimated cost	Actual cost
Rings		
Bride	$_____	$_____
Groom	$_____	$_____
Engraving	$_____	$_____
Other	$_____	$_____
Bridalwear		
Wedding gown/dress	$_____	$_____
Alterations	$_____	$_____
Headpiece/veil	$_____	$_____
Undergarments	$_____	$_____
Shoes	$_____	$_____
Purse	$_____	$_____
Garter	$_____	$_____
Other	$_____	$_____
Groom's Attire		
Tuxedo or formalwear	$_____	$_____
Shoes	$_____	$_____
Other	$_____	$_____
Attendants' Attire		
Bridesmaids' dresses	$_____	$_____
Bridesmaids' shoes	$_____	$_____
Groomsmen's formalwear	$_____	$_____
Groomsmen's shoes	$_____	$_____
Flower girl's dress	$_____	$_____
Ring-bearer's attire	$_____	$_____
Ring-bearer's pillow	$_____	$_____

	Estimated cost	Actual cost
Officiant and Legalities		
Officiant's fee	$_____	$_____
Marriage license	$_____	$_____
Blood tests (if required)	$_____	$_____
Other	$_____	$_____
Invitations/Stationery		
Invitations	$_____	$_____
Calligraphy	$_____	$_____
RSVP cards	$_____	$_____
Thank-you cards	$_____	$_____
Postage	$_____	$_____
Itineraries	$_____	$_____
Announcement in paper	$_____	$_____
Flowers		
Bride's bouquet	$_____	$_____
Bridesmaids' bouquets	$_____	$_____
Flower girl's flowers	$_____	$_____
Boutonnieres	$_____	$_____
Corsages	$_____	$_____
Flowers for church	$_____	$_____
Flowers for reception	$_____	$_____
Other	$_____	$_____
Beauty		
Hair stylist	$_____	$_____
Makeup	$_____	$_____
Manicure/Pedicure	$_____	$_____
Other	$_____	$_____

	Estimated cost	Actual cost
Photographer/Videographer		
Sitting fee	$_____	$_____
Wedding photos	$_____	$_____
Albums	$_____	$_____
Gift sets	$_____	$_____
Videographer fee	$_____	$_____
Video/DVD copies	$_____	$_____
Other	$_____	$_____
Transportation		
Limousine or bridal car	$_____	$_____
Attendant's cars	$_____	$_____
Guest transportation	$_____	$_____
Alternate (e.g. carriage)	$_____	$_____
Other	$_____	$_____

	Estimated cost	*Actual cost*
Reception		
Venue fee	$_____	$_____
Catering fee	$_____	$_____
Food	$_____	$_____
Beverages	$_____	$_____
Champagne	$_____	$_____
Cake	$_____	$_____
Cake knife	$_____	$_____
Decorations	$_____	$_____
Table centerpieces	$_____	$_____
Favors	$_____	$_____
Rentals (tent, etc.)	$_____	$_____
Music/DJ	$_____	$_____
Toasting glasses	$_____	$_____
Other	$_____	$_____
Miscellaneous Expenses		
Wedding planner fees	$_____	$_____
Other	$_____	$_____
Honeymoon Expenses		
Passports	$_____	$_____
Visas	$_____	$_____
Inoculations	$_____	$_____
Airfare	$_____	$_____
Transportation (car rental)	$_____	$_____
Hotel	$_____	$_____
Entertainment	$_____	$_____
Meals	$_____	$_____
Other	$_____	$_____

2.3 Getting Organized

In order to pull off a successful wedding you will have to find ways to stay on-time and on-track, and assign or delegate responsibility to others.

As a wedding planner it is very important to prepare a time-line schedule and checklists, to ensure that everything gets planned with sufficient time and nothing is missed or forgotten. Ideally, it is beneficial to have a full year to put together a wedding to ensure that venues are available, etc., however; it is not essential.

2.3.1 Preparing a Time-Line Schedule

A sample *Wedding Time-Line Schedule and Checklist* begins on the next page for your use and reference. It has been prepared based on having a full year to plan a wedding. You may wish to revise the timing and list somewhat if you have a different amount of time to work with, and if there are different items you have agreed to co-ordinate.

After you have reworked the schedule for your current clients, you should then either write down the items to be handled in a daytimer or on a calendar, insert the information into a simple Excel or similar spread-sheet program, or put it into an electronic organizer such as a Palm Pilot. Another alternative is to use wedding scheduling software, which is covered in section 5.2.3 of this guide.

Nancy Freedman (also known as The Task Mistress), is founder of **TheTaskMistress.com**, a New York based company that takes care of handling many different tasks for busy individuals (including planning weddings from time to time). Nancy advises that it is best to select an organizational system that works for you. She says:

> "I think one has to find which elements of organization work best for them. Whether you use a handheld device or a book, or if you are an old-fashioned list maker, have that available at all times. Don't be afraid to call to follow up. I heard about a wedding where the ice had not been delivered. To add insult to injury, the wedding was held outside during the summer."

Wedding Time-Line Schedule and Checklist

12 Months Before

❑ Attend consultation with the bride and groom

❑ Have the couple complete Wedding Registration Form

❑ Have bride and groom select bridal party and other attendants and ask them to participate in their wedding

❑ Provide bride and groom with wedding etiquette information (as required)

❑ Have bride and groom finalize wedding date

❑ Prepare budget and review it with bride and groom

❑ Book ceremony venue and pay deposit

❑ Book reception venue and pay deposit

❑ Determine if venues require proof of liability insurance and, if so, arrange same

❑ Have bride and groom prepare list of guests to attend

❑ Co-ordinate engagement party, if requested

10-11 Months Before

❑ Determine what customs and/or traditions, personalized vows, readings and/or exchanges the bride and groom would like to include at the ceremony (e.g. lighting of unity candle, flowers to mothers, etc.)

❑ Have bride and groom select and meet with wedding officiant (with you)

❑ Book caterer

❑ Book musicians for the ceremony (e.g. soloist, organist, etc.)

❑ Book musicians for the reception (band, DJ, etc.)

❑ Book photographer

❑ Book videographer

8-9 Months Before

❑ Book florist

❑ Book cake designer/baker

❑ Book transportation for wedding

❑ Have bride and groom sign up for premarital counseling (optional)

❑ Have bride select and purchase wedding dress, head-piece/veil, shoes, lingerie and accessories

❑ Have bride select bridesmaids' and flower girl's dresses and accessories

6-7 Months Before

❑ Make arrangements to have bridesmaids and flower girl fitted for dresses

❑ Have mothers of the bride and groom select their dresses

❑ Have bride and groom sign up with a gift registry and select desired gifts

❑ Book calligrapher

❑ Book rentals (such as tents, tables, chairs, linens, china, glassware, cake knife, toasting glasses, candelabras, etc., as required)

❑ Have bride and groom send any required deposits to vendors/suppliers

❑ Remind bride and groom to book their honeymoon and update passports, obtain visas and any inoculations required

❑ Reserve rooms for out-of-town guests (if requested)

❑ Review all vendors/suppliers contracts and provide advice to bride and groom

5 Months Before

❑ Order invitations, RSVP cards, thank-you cards, itineraries, etc.

❑ Select and order all flowers

❑ Plan reception including finalizing theme and décor, select favors, table centerpieces, decorations, candles, etc.

❑ Have bride and groom finalize the selections of ceremony music

❑ Have bride and groom finalize the selections of reception music

❑ Provide music requests and lists to all musicians

❑ Have bride and groom finalize wedding invitation list

4 Months Before

❑ Review budget with bride and groom to ensure it is on track

❑ Remind bride and groom to select their wedding rings and arrange for engravings

❑ Have groom select and get fitted for tuxedo or alternative formalwear and shoes

❑ Have groomsmen (and possibly ring-bearer and ushers) fitted for tuxedos or alternative formalwear and shoes

❑ Meet with caterer (with bride and groom) for tastings and to find out menu options

❑ Order wedding cake and groom's cake (if desired)

❑ Have bride and groom arrange for emcee and other speakers (e.g. individuals making toasts) at the reception

❑ Have bride and groom select and arrange with individual to handle guest book

❑ Have bride and groom select and arrange with individuals to hand out programs

❑ Talk to maid of honor and best man about planning a bridal shower and bachelor party

❑ Have bride and groom book honeymoon suite for wedding night

❑ Have bride book suite to get ready in on the day of the wedding, if applicable

❑ Have bride and groom make arrangements for the planning of a rehearsal dinner and day-after-wedding brunch

3 Months Before

❑ Have bride make all appointments for hair, makeup and manicure/pedicure

❑ Have bride and groom get blood tests and/or have medical examinations, if required

❑ Provide caterer with food/menu and beverage selections

❑ Plan additional liquor needs, if required

❑ Have bride and groom select any readings (and readers) for the ceremony

❑ Have bride and groom meet with the officiant to review ceremony and finalize vows

❑ Determine what customs and/or traditions the bride and groom would like to include at the reception (such as formal cake cutting, toasts, etc.)

❑ Finalize time and location of rehearsal

❑ Prepare maps, directions, information sheets and hotel recommendations for out-of-town guests

❑ Prepare wedding program, wedding weekend itinerary and wedding day schedule

❑ Obtain wedding invitation list from couple

❑ Provide wedding list to calligrapher

❑ Meet with stationer to have invitations, RSVP cards, thank-you cards, itineraries, programs, menus, etc. and any accessories such as napkins printed

2 Months Before

❏ Pick up and mail out wedding invitations (together with RSVP cards, etc.)

❏ Contact booked venues to confirm arrangements and arrange with bride and groom to pay balances owing, as required

❏ Have bride and bridesmaids attend follow-up wedding attire fittings

❏ Prepare information and instruction sheets for all members of the bridal party and for all vendors

❏ Have bride prepare guest list for shower and give to maid of honor

❏ Have groom prepare guest list for groom's get together and give to best man

❏ Have bride select going away outfit

1 Month Before

❏ Have bride and groom obtain marriage license (within legal time period required)

❏ Track gifts received and send out thank-you cards (if requested to handle this)

❏ Have bride and groom pick up wedding rings and ensure they fit

❏ Provide photographer with list of photos to be taken

❏ Provide instructions to videographer

❏ Confirm music lists and arrangements with musicians

❏ Confirm transportation arrangements

❏ Confirm flower order and arrangements with florist

❏ Confirm rental requirements and drop-off times

❏ Pick up any ceremony or reception accessories not provided by rental company or caterer (e.g. candles, goblets, ring pillow, guest book, cake knife, etc.)

❏ Have bride and groom purchase gifts for bridal attendants, parents, ushers and each other

3 Weeks Before

❏ Follow up with guests who haven't sent in an RSVP

❏ Prepare seating plan for reception

❏ Prepare name plates/seating cards

❏ Have bride go in for trial hair and makeup appointment(s) and confirm wedding day appointments

❏ Have bride and groom prepare a wedding reception toast/speech

2 Weeks Before

❏ Provide wedding day schedule and instructions to all appropriate vendors

❏ Phone to confirm all arrangements with vendors and suppliers one more time

❏ Have bride and bridesmaids pick up their gowns/dresses and all accessories (including veil and/or headpiece for bride, shoes, jewelry, etc.)

❏ Have couple pick up tickets, itinerary, travelers' checks, etc. for honeymoon

❏ Have bride arrange bridesmaids' luncheon and give gifts to attendants

❏ Have groom arrange groomsmen get together and give gifts to attendants

1 Week Before

❏ Provide caterer with final numbers for reception

❏ Confirm the rehearsal date and time with all members of the bridal party and all others assisting with the wedding (such as officiant, parents, photographer, videographer, musicians, etc.)

❏ Meet with bride and groom to review all wedding plans and to get the marriage license from them

❏ Find out from bride and groom where wedding gifts that are received on day of wedding are to be dropped off

❏ Obtain from bride and groom the final checks for vendors' outstanding fees (such as musicians, officiant, caterer, florist, transportation, and your fees, etc.)

❏ Prepare envelopes addressed to various vendors to pay final fees

❏ Have bride and groom pack for their honeymoon including clothes, toiletries, tickets, passports, visas, maps, guide books, travelers checks, money, etc.

❏ Have bride and groom pack their going away outfits, wedding night and next day clothes and toiletries

2 Days Before Wedding

❑ Have groom and groomsmen pick up tuxedos/formalwear

❑ Have bride and groom give gifts to parents and to each other

❑ Pack all items you need to bring to the wedding ceremony (such as guest book and pen, marriage license, ceremony programs, candles, emergency kit, etc.)

❑ Drop off all reception favors, table centerpieces, cake knife, toasting goblets, candles, etc. at reception venue so they can be set up prior to reception

❑ Have couple confirm early meeting times with bridal party for the wedding day

Day Before Wedding/Rehearsal

❑ Attend and direct rehearsal

❑ Hand out wedding schedule, itineraries and instructions to all members of the bridal party and any others involved with the wedding.

❑ Provide seating details to ushers

❑ Bring ring-bearer's pillow and provide to individual responsible for ring-bearer

❑ Have groom give bride's ring to best man (or to you, for safekeeping, if a ring-bearer is involved in the wedding)

❑ Have bride give groom's ring to maid of honor (or to you, for safekeeping, if a ring-bearer is involved)

❑ Oversee the decorating of the ceremony venue and the reception venue

Day of Wedding (Prior to Ceremony)

❑ Bring your charged cell phone with you for the day

❑ Bring your checklists, schedule, list of vendors and contact information including phone numbers

❑ Attend with bride, as required (and make sure she gets something to eat)

❑ Oversee and co-ordinate with venue manager, musicians, photographer, videographer, officiant, florist, decorator, transportation company (if required), etc.

❑ Bring marriage license, guest book and pen, programs and candles (and set everything up)

❑ Bring emergency kit (small sewing kit, safety pins, bobby pins, antacid, aspirin, Kleenex, brush, hairspray, etc.) in case needed

Day of Wedding (Ceremony and After)

❑ Attend and oversee ceremony (including processional, recessional and receiving line after ceremony) and provide supervision, guidance, support, assistance, instructions, or whatever may be required to have the ceremony run smoothly

❑ Provide final payment checks to all ceremony vendors

❑ Collect marriage license, candles, guest book and pen, extra programs and anything left behind after the ceremony

❑ Attend photo-taking after ceremony and co-ordinate with photographer

Day of Wedding (Reception)

❏ Oversee and co-ordinate with venue manager, caterer, musicians, DJ, cake designer, photographer, videographer, etc.

❏ Co-ordinate and oversee reception receiving line

❏ Provide final payment checks to all reception vendors/ suppliers

❏ Co-ordinate first dance(s), cake cutting, bouquet throwing, garter toss, etc. (as requested)

❏ Collect all wedding gifts and cash received at reception and deliver them to pre-determined location

After the Wedding

❏ Drop off wedding dress at cleaners (if requested)

❏ Return groom's formalwear attire (if requested)

❏ Arrange for pressing of flowers (if requested)

❏ Send wedding announcement to the newspaper (if requested)

❏ Send out wedding announcement cards (if requested)

❏ Send out thank-you cards for gifts (if requested)

❏ Send out change of address cards (if requested)

❏ Ensure that bride and groom receive marriage license

❏ Send a congratulations and "thank you for your business" card to the couple

2.3.2 Preparing Checklists

To stay organized as a wedding planner, checklists are a must because they will assist you with keeping track of what has already been handled and what still needs to be done.

Besides having a thorough checklist for yourself to follow, it is also helpful to provide the bride and groom with a checklist for any items they will need to arrange. This will not only help to ensure that the bride and groom take care of everything that needs to be handled by them, but it will also clarify what items you are **not** handling for them so that nothing gets missed or forgotten.

A sample checklist for the bride and groom follows on pages 47-54. You may wish to revise this list, depending on what services you will be providing, or use it as a starting point to create your own checklist for the bride and groom. Other planning checklists can be found online at websites such as **AmericanBridal.com** and **WeddingChannel.com**.

Checklist for the Bride and Groom

12 Months Before

- ❏ Announce engagement in the newspaper (if desired)

- ❏ Send out engagement announcements (if desired)

- ❏ Plan an engagement party (if desired)

- ❏ Discuss wedding arrangements with parents

- ❏ Determine if parents will be assisting with the wedding costs

- ❏ Meet with wedding planner to begin wedding preparations and decide on style and theme of wedding

- ❏ Finalize wedding date

- ❏ Decide on ceremony and reception venues

- ❏ Select bridal party and other attendants and ask them to participate in your wedding

- ❏ Prepare invitation list

10-11 Months Before

- ❏ Determine what customs and/or traditions, personalized vows, readings and/or exchanges you would like to include at the ceremony (e.g. lighting of unity candle, flowers to mothers, etc.)

- ❏ Select and meet with wedding officiant

8-9 Months Before

❏ Sign up for premarital counseling, if required

❏ Bride to select and purchase wedding dress, headpiece/ veil, shoes, lingerie and accessories

❏ Bride to select bridesmaids and flower girl dresses and accessories

6-7 Months Before

❏ Make arrangements to have bridesmaids and flower girl fitted with dresses

❏ Have mothers select their dresses

❏ Get listed at a gift registry and select desired gifts

❏ Provide any required deposits for vendors

❏ Begin planning and booking honeymoon including air, transportation, hotels and entertainment and update passports, obtain visas and any inoculations required

❏ Reserve rooms for out-of-town guests

❏ Arrange with a family member or friend to finalize out-of-town accommodations, as required

❏ Sign all vendors/suppliers contracts (after reviewed by wedding planner)

5 Months Before

❏ Select invitation design

❏ Select ceremony music

❑ Select reception music and prepare list of requests

❑ Finalize wedding invitation list

4 Months Before

❑ Review budget with wedding planner to ensure on track

❑ Purchase wedding rings and arrange for engravings

❑ Groom to select and get fitted for tuxedo or alternative formalwear and shoes

❑ Have groomsmen (and possibly ring-bearer and ushers) fitted for tuxedos or alternative formalwear including shoes

❑ Meet with caterer (with wedding planner) for tastings and to find out menu options

❑ Select all flowers for the wedding

❑ Select an emcee and decide on other speakers (e.g. individuals making toasts) at the reception and ask these individuals about performing these duties

❑ Select and arrange with individual(s) to handle guest book at ceremony and reception

❑ Select and arrange with individual(s) to hand out wedding ceremony programs

❑ Reserve honeymoon suite for wedding night

❑ Bride to reserve getting-ready suite for the day of the wedding, if required

❑ Make arrangements for the planning of a rehearsal dinner and day-after-wedding brunch, if desired

3 Months Before

❏ Bride to make all appointments for hair, makeup and mani-cure/pedicure for wedding

❏ Get blood tests and/or have medical examinations, if re-quired

❏ Finalize food/menu and beverage selections

❏ Select any readings (and readers) for the ceremony

❏ Meet with the officiant to review ceremony and finalize vows

❏ Determine what customs and/or traditions you would like to include at the reception (such as formal cake cutting, toasts, etc.)

❏ Finalize time and location of rehearsal

❏ Provide finalized wedding invitation list to wedding plan-ner

2 Months Before

❏ Bride and bridesmaids to attend follow-up wedding attire fittings

❏ Bride to prepare guest list for shower and give to maid of honor

❏ Groom to prepare guest list for groom's get together and give to best man

❏ Bride to select going away outfit

1 Month Before

❑ Obtain marriage license (within legal time period required)

❑ Send out thank-you cards for gifts received or advise wedding planner of gifts received so that she can send out thank-you cards

❑ Pick up wedding rings; ensure they fit and are engraved

❑ Finalize lists of photos to be taken and video to be shot and provide these to wedding planner

❑ Purchase gifts for bridal attendants, parents, ushers and each other

3 Weeks Before

❑ Advise wedding planner of any special seating arrangements for reception

❑ Bride to go in for trial hair and makeup appointment(s) and confirm wedding day appointments

❑ Prepare wedding reception toast/speech

❑ Update insurance policies (life, household, car, etc.)

❑ Complete change of name/change of address paperwork

❑ Open joint bank account (if desired)

❑ Select individual to arrange for return of groom's formalwear attire

❑ Select individual to drop off bridal gown at the cleaners

❑ Select individual to take flowers to be pressed

2 Weeks Before

❑ Bride and bridesmaids to pick up their gowns/dresses and all accessories (including veil and/or headpiece for bride, lingerie for bride, shoes, jewelry, etc.)

❑ Bride to decide on wearing something old, something new, something borrowed and something blue on wedding day

❑ Pick up all tickets, itinerary, travelers' checks, etc. for honeymoon

❑ Provide honeymoon details to close friend or family member

❑ Bride to arrange bridesmaids' luncheon and give gifts to attendants

❑ Groom to arrange groomsmen get together and give gifts to attendants

❑ Groom to get hair cut

1 Week Before

❑ Meet with the wedding planner to review all wedding plans and to supply the marriage license

❑ Advise wedding planner where wedding gifts and cash that are received on day of wedding are to be dropped off

❑ Prepare final checks for vendors' fees (such as musicians, officiant, caterer, florist and wedding planner fees, etc.) and provide these to the wedding planner

❑ Pack for honeymoon including clothes, toiletries, tickets, passports, visas, maps, guide books, travelers checks, money, etc.

❑ Pack for wedding night including going away outfits, wedding night clothes and next day clothes and toiletries

❑ Arrange for temporary stoppage of newspaper and mail while away on honeymoon

2 Days Before Wedding

❑ Groom and his attendants to pick up tuxedos/formalwear

❑ Bride to get manicure/pedicure

❑ Give gifts to parents and to each other

❑ Confirm early meeting times with bridal party for the day of the wedding

Day Before Wedding/Rehearsal

❑ Attend rehearsal (plan to arrive about 20 minutes early)

❑ Groom to give bride's ring to best man (or to wedding planner, for safekeeping, if a ring-bearer is involved in the wedding)

❑ Bride to give groom's ring to maid of honor (or to wedding planner, for safekeeping, if a ring-bearer is involved in the wedding)

❑ Attend wedding rehearsal dinner/party

Day of Wedding (Prior to Ceremony)

❑ Wake up with plenty of time to get ready for your special day

❑ Remember to eat

❑ Bride to get hair and makeup done

❑ Get dressed

❑ Bride wears something old, something new, something borrowed, something blue

❑ Bride to wear garter (if desired)

❑ Get to the ceremony venue on time

Day of Wedding (Ceremony and after)

❑ Enjoy the day!

Day of Wedding (Reception)

❑ Enjoy the evening!

After the Wedding

❑ Send wedding announcement to the newspaper

❑ Send out wedding announcement cards

❑ Send out thank-you cards for gifts

❑ Send out change of address cards

❑ Complete any name change paperwork

❑ Get marriage license from wedding planner

❑ Pick up wedding dress from cleaners

❑ Pick up pressed flowers

❑ Update wills

2.3.3 Keeping a Wedding Organizer

Another way to stay organized is by keeping a *wedding organizer* for each wedding you are working on. Also known as a *wedding binder* or *wedding planner*, a wedding organizer is a binder containing all the documents that you need for the wedding.

It is a great way of keeping together and carrying around all the paperwork that you will require for vendor, client, or venue meetings and on the wedding day itself. It is like a "manual of operations" for the wedding (some wedding planners call it their "bible.")

A good-quality attractive three-ring binder will do nicely, and to make life even simpler you can buy paper that is three-hole pre-punched and plastic cover sheets or dividers that are also pre-punched. The documents you will want to include in the binder are:

- A copy of the contract between your company and your client

- Copies of all the vendor contracts

- Wedding overview

- Event schedules

- Contact list

Wedding Overview

From your initial client consultation and resulting meetings you will create a contract outlining exactly which package your clients want and what services you will provide (you can find a sample contract in chapter 5). From this information you should create a *Wedding Overview* detailing dates, places and times of every event within the contracted package. An example of a Wedding Overview appears on page 58.

Event Schedules

You will notice this general overview does not include particulars like attendees, directions or duration. These and any other relevant details will be included in the *Event Schedules* (or whatever name you've given).

Sample Event Schedule

L. Smith – C. Jones Wedding
Rehearsal Dinner Schedule
Friday, August 12, 2005
6:30 p.m.–10:00 p.m.
Ricardo's Restaurante, 482 Park Lane
Contact: 555-1234 (Vincente)

Time:	9:00 a.m.
Responsible:	Krista
Location:	Office
Task:	Call Vincente with final head count.
Notes:	Check answering machine and email for last-minute RSVPs.

Time:	9:00 a.m.–9:15 a.m.
Responsible:	Krista
Location:	Office
Task:	Discuss last-minute menu changes with Vincente.
Notes:	Check RSVP list for special dietary concerns.

Time:	3:30 p.m.–4:00 p.m.
Responsible:	Wendy
Location:	Blooming Beautiful (130 10th Ave.)
Task:	Pick up flowers for table settings.
Notes:	Ordered 1 large Calla Lily table arrangement, 2 small assorted table arrangements (contact: Yolanda).

Time:	4:00 p.m.–4:45 p.m.
Responsible:	Wendy
Location:	Ricardo's
Task:	Deliver flowers to Ricardo's.
Notes:	Park in back. Ring buzzer. Large arrangement to be placed in the middle of the table with the two small arrangements on either side.

Time:	6:00 p.m.
Responsible:	Wendy
Location:	Ricardo's
Task:	Check table settings and arrange place cards.
Notes:	Seating arrangement attached to Ricardo's contract.

Rehearsal Dinner Schedule (continued)

Time:	10:00 p.m.
Responsible:	Wendy
Location:	Ricardo's
Task:	Settle bill. Discuss event with Vincente.
Notes:	Final bill to be paid by Cyril Smith, father of the groom.

Regardless of the name you give to this important part of your binder, it should at least contain the following elements:

- The name of the bride and groom (e.g. Smith – Jones Wedding) and the actual wedding date should appear on each page

- A brief description of each task

- The time of day each task will take place

- The location (including address and directions if necessary)

- Who is responsible for each task

- Any other important details

You should do a separate Event Schedule for each event within the entire Wedding Package you are contracted for. An event schedule for a rehearsal dinner could look something like the example shown on these two pages.

A similar system should be followed for each event in the package and become part of the wedding organizer. The event schedule for the actual wedding and reception will, of course, include many more items than those included in the above illustration.

Another very important part of every wedding organizer is a contact list of telephone numbers for everyone involved in the planning or execution of the wedding. Include phone numbers for the vendors supplying goods and services and backup emergency cellular phone numbers.

Sample Wedding Overview

Client:
Wedding Date:

Vendor Meetings
Vendor: _____   Address: _____
Date: _____   _____
Time: _____   _____

Vendor: _____   Address: _____
Date: _____   _____
Time: _____   _____

Bridesmaids' Luncheon
Venue: _____   Address: _____
Date: _____   _____
Time: _____   _____

Rehearsal
Venue: _____   Address: _____
Date: _____   _____
Time: _____   _____

Rehearsal Dinner
Venue: _____   Address: _____
Date: _____   _____
Time: _____   _____

Wedding
Venue: _____   Address: _____
Date: _____   _____
Time: _____   _____

Reception
Venue: _____   Address: _____
Date: _____   _____
Time: _____   _____

Gift Opening
Venue: _____   Address: _____
Date: _____   _____
Time: _____   _____

2.4 Planning the Ceremony

Getting married is a major rite of passage in a person's life, and because of this the most meaningful part of the wedding day for the bride and groom is likely to be the ceremony. Although the reception is a fun and significant part of the day, it is essentially a celebratory party, while the ceremony is an emotional exchange of commitment, love, and promises with personal touches special to the bride and groom.

In your initial consultation with the bride and groom (and from the Wedding Registration Form completed by the couple), you will gather information such as the number of people attending, the desired style of the ceremony (traditional or non-traditional), the color scheme, whether any special exchanges or personalized vows are desired, etc.

After you have obtained this information, you will then be in a good position to start the planning. There are many different items that need to be decided upon and arranged for a ceremony. This section covers the basics of planning a ceremony, including:

- Selecting the wedding date

- Selecting the venue

- Selecting the officiant

- Selecting ceremony vows, exchanges and readings

- Selecting ceremony music

- Obtaining the marriage license

- Ceremony rehearsal

- The ceremony processional, recessional and receiving line

- Other ceremony arrangements

In addition to the information provided in this guide, it is suggested that you also take the time to read wedding books that focus mainly on the ceremony to enhance your knowledge about various customs, religious rituals, traditions, etc.

One recommended book that can provide you with more detailed information about ceremonies (vows, rituals, traditions, readings, etc.) is *The Knot Guide to Wedding Vows and Traditions: Readings, Rituals, Music, Dances, Speeches and Toasts*, by Carley Roney.

2.4.1 Selecting the Wedding Date

When your clients meet with you for the initial consultation, it is quite likely that they will already have a date in mind for their wedding or, if not, they will at least have a particular month that they wish to get married in.

If the couple is set on a particular date for one reason or another, then they may need to be flexible about the venue or officiant they choose for their wedding. However, if a venue location is more important than the date, the couple may need to be flexible about the date. It is ideal if your clients can select two tentative wedding dates so that there is a backup if the first (preferred) date is not available.

Considerations in Choosing a Date

There are some things your clients may want to take into consideration when they are finalizing their wedding date. Although the vast majority of weddings are held on a Saturday in either Spring or Summer (June being the most popular month), there is no requirement to stick to this day or time of year.

 In fact, weddings held on a day other than a Saturday – and those held in off-season months – will be less expensive and easier to plan. Exceptions to these are weddings held at Christmas time or on Valentine's Day (which is an extremely popular time to get married.)

Another thing that your clients will need to take into consideration is that a number of venues and officiants can be booked up to one year (and sometimes even more) in advance of a Saturday in Spring or Summer. Accordingly, it is helpful to have at least a full year to plan the wedding if a popular venue or officiant are desired. Some additional things your clients should keep in mind before booking a date are:

- Holidays such as Easter, Thanksgiving, Christmas, etc., because travel will likely be overpriced and difficult for some guests during these times of the year

- Events (annual, special, or major sporting events) that take place in the area of the wedding. It is ideal to avoid planning the wedding during these times because chances are accommodation will be difficult to obtain and more expensive than normal

- Religious restrictions (if applicable) that may rule out certain days

- Family commitments such as graduations, other weddings, big birthday celebrations, etc.

- What the weather might be like during the time of year desired

It is important to have your clients finalize the wedding date as soon as possible so that you can assist them with planning the rest of their wedding. Once the date is known, then a venue can be reserved, the officiant can be booked and so on.

2.4.2 Selecting the Venue

If the bride and groom are practicing members of a religious faith, it is highly likely that they will want to get married in their place of worship. However, if you have clients who are not members of a particular religion or who want a non-traditional wedding, the bride and groom may already have an idea in mind of where they want to get married or they may ask you for some ideas.

Following are some suggestions for where a ceremony could be held:

- A place that is unique and special to the couple (for example, the location where they first met or where they got engaged, etc.)

- Amusement park

- Art gallery

- Back yard of couple, family member or friend

- Beach

- Boat

- Botanical gardens

- City hall

- Community hall

- Country club

- Country inn

- Courthouse or judge's chambers

- Historical site

- Hotel

- Mountain

- Museum

- Non-denominational church

- Park

- Outdoors (anywhere) in a large tent

- Resort location (e.g. Disneyworld, Las Vegas, Caribbean)

- Restaurant

- Victorian mansion

- Wedding chapel

- Winery

- Zoo

The ideas listed above are for weddings to be held in North America. Fortunately, in North America, there are very few restrictions as to where a couple can get married. However, if you are planning a wedding abroad, this may not necessarily be the case. Prior to booking a ceremony venue abroad, ensure that the laws allow a marriage to legally take place in the chosen venue.

UK Wedding Restrictions

In England, prior to 1995, if a couple was not affiliated with a particular church, the only other option for the bride and groom was to get married at a register office.

Approximately seven years ago one of the co-authors of this guide planned a wedding in England. At that time the laws had relaxed somewhat and couples could also choose to get married at one of the few hotels or historical sites that were approved for marriage ceremonies by the government ("approved premises" as they are officially known). Each year since that time, many more locations have been added to the "approved premises" list and now there are about 3,700 approved premises throughout England and Wales.

It is important to note that if a couple is not married at a register office or at an "approved premise" or in a church in England or Wales, the marriage is not considered legal.

Finding a Venue

A website that lists venues throughout the world is Confetti Venues at **www.confetti.co.uk/venues/default.asp**. To locate possible wedding venues in North America, check with the local chamber of commerce, local visitors bureau or parks department to find out if they have any information on facilities that may be available for wedding ceremonies.

Alternatively, you can search for venues on the Internet by entering in the terms "wedding venue" and the name of your city. (Chapter 4 has some additional links plus a list of top resort locations.)

If your clients want a non-denominational marriage in a church, one option is to contact the Unitarian Universalist Association to find a Unitarian church in your area. If you have access to the Internet you can browse the complete directory at: **www.uua.org**.

If you would prefer to have a hard copy of the directory which is updated yearly you may also order it directly from their online bookstore or contact them by mail, phone or fax. At the time of printing, this guide was $25 U.S. plus shipping.

Unitarian Universalist Association
25 Beacon Street
Boston, MA 02108
Phone: 1-800-215-9076
Fax: (617) 723-4805

Questions to Ask

Once a desired venue has been chosen, before you book it, it is advisable to thoroughly check out the venue (with your clients) and find out the following:

- What is the fee for renting the venue and what does the fee include?

- How much deposit is required and when is the rest of the fee payable?

- How long can the venue be used for at that fee?

- What are the hourly charges if the time allotted is exceeded?

- Is there a security deposit required?

- What is the refund policy?

- What are the insurance requirements, if any?

- Can the venue be used for a rehearsal the day/evening before the wedding (and is this included within the rental fee)?

- Will there be a venue co-ordinator available, if required? If so, what are the duties of the venue co-ordinator?

- Are there any officiant options with the venue?

- Are there any requirements regarding an officiant?

- Is pre-marriage counseling required (if in a place of worship)?

- Can couples from mixed faiths be married at the venue (if applicable)?

- What rental equipment is included with the fee (for example, microphones, candelabras, stereo system, organ, etc.) or, what is the cost of using these if not included within the fee?

- Is there an organist or pianist available?

- What is the room capacity?

- Is there a change room/waiting room that is included for use?

- What parking is available?

- Will there be any other weddings held on the desired date?

- If any other weddings are planned, what time will they be held at?

- How long before the wedding can the florist and decorator come in to set up?

- Are there any restrictions with respect to decorating?

- Are there any wedding policies or rules (for example, rules regarding picture taking or petal, rice or birdseed tossing, etc.)?

To ensure that you don't forget to ask any questions, it is advisable that you print off a list of these questions and take them with you and make notes while reviewing the venue and discussing the rental of it with the venue co-ordinator. If your clients decide to proceed with the venue, request that the venue co-ordinator reserve the venue for your clients and also request that a rental contract be prepared that covers all items that have been agreed upon. This will help avoid any misunderstandings or surprises.

As part of your role as a wedding planner, once the contract is prepared, you should review it to ensure that everything is included and then arrange with your clients to sign the contract and provide any deposits that are required to keep the booking.

Venue Insurance

At some venues (such as museums, art galleries or venues where you may also be holding the reception), you may need to obtain insurance. The average cost for wedding insurance ranges from about $100 – $200.

If obtained by the bride and groom, wedding insurance can be taken out as a rider on their existing insurance policy. Another option for wedding insurance is for your clients to purchase "wedding specific" insurance from a wedding insurance provider (note that different policies will cover different components of a wedding).

You can find various providers on the Internet by going to your favorite search engine and searching for "wedding insurance"; or your clients can obtain wedding insurance through RV Nuccio & Associates Weddingsurance program by visiting **www.rvnuccio.com** or phoning 1-800-ENGAGED.

Ensure that you check out whichever company (if any) is chosen to provide insurance with the Better Business Bureau. Also, review the insurance policy to determine what is included before your clients go ahead with the insurance purchase.

2.4.3 Selecting the Officiant

If your clients are members of a religious faith, they will likely want to choose an officiant from their place of worship. However, if your clients are inactive in their faith or if they have no religious affiliations they may need some guidance and assistance from you to select an officiant for their wedding.

Some choices for officiants are:

- Minister, priest, rabbi, bishop or clergymember at place of worship

- Ordained minister or clergymember from a non-denominational church

- Justice of the Peace

- Judge

- Captain of a ship

- Marriage Commissioners (in Canada)

Depending on where the marriage will take place, some of the following may also have the authority to perform marriages:

- County clerks

- Court clerks

- Mayor (of your city)

- Notary public

Whoever is selected to perform the ceremony must be someone who can legally perform the marriage in the location where the couple is being married. After all, the officiant will need to complete all the legal paperwork for the marriage to be valid.

Each jurisdiction has different regulations or laws regarding who can perform marriages so it is important to find out the laws. You can do this by checking with your local marriage license bureau (you can find them by phoning your city hall and asking where marriage licenses can be attained) or you may be able to find them in your phone book in the government listings section.

It is ideal for the couple to select an officiant who they like and feel comfortable with and who will work with the couple and allow them to have a ceremony that is right for them. The best way to find this out is to set up a meeting between your clients, the officiant, and yourself to discuss the officant's services. At this meeting, you will discuss the ceremony, vows, exchanges, readings, prayers, music, etc. and get agreement for anything special desired by your clients.

It is best to do this before the officiant is hired (and definitely well in advance of the rehearsal, because by that time if the officiant is not agreeable to your clients' desires, it is too late to make any changes).

Officiants typically charge from $50 to more than $300 to perform a marriage ceremony. The fees may be higher if the officiant is requested to travel to your clients' preferred location to perform the marriage (instead of having the ceremony performed at the officiant's location).

Questions to Ask

- What is their fee and when is it payable?

- What is the refund policy if the wedding needs to be postponed?

- How many times will the officiant meet with the couple prior to the wedding?

- Is the officiant agreeable to co-ordinating the ceremony with you (the wedding planner) as well as with the couple?

- Does the officiant's fee include the rehearsal (preferably the day or night before the wedding)?

- Does the officiant have any rules or procedures they need to follow when performing a wedding ceremony?

- Are there any restrictions with respect to the music, prayers, readings, etc.?

- How are interfaith marriages handled?

- Will the officiant perform a marriage in conjunction with another officiant?

- Will the officiant perform the ceremony at another location?

- Will the officiant provide a copy of the ceremony script beforehand (if this has not already been obtained)?

- Can changes be made to the script?

- Can personal vows be included within the ceremony?

- Will the officiant attend the reception?

Finding an Officiant

To find a non-denominational/civil officiant in your area, contact your local marriage license bureau and ask if they have a listing of civil officiants that can be hired. To find a non-denominational officiant in Canada, look in the Yellow Pages for "Marriage Commissioners." You may also be able to find an officiant online. **WeddingOfficiants.com** is a website that provides a matching service for brides and grooms with officiants in their area.

After an officiant is selected, it is advisable to book the officiant as soon as possible. Once again, make sure that a contract is put in place that covers all items agreed to. After you have reviewed the contract, arrange for the couple to sign it and pay any deposit required to ensure that the officiant is reserved for your clients' wedding.

2.4.4 Ceremony Vows, Exchanges and Readings

If your clients are of a religious faith and choose to be married within their place of worship, there will most likely be customs, traditions and rituals that need to be included within their ceremony.

Each denomination will have its own rules, requirements and procedures relating to wedding ceremonies. Some will allow for variances and personal touches, while others may be quite restrictive. One thing to keep in mind, though, is that it is important that the ceremony and vows are reflective of your clients' feelings and beliefs.

Most wedding ceremonies contain the following common elements (though this may vary depending on the religion, officiant, or the bride and groom's desires):

- A greeting

- Statement of intentions and wedding vows

- Exchange of rings

- Readings and blessings

- Pronouncement of husband and wife

The most common denominational weddings held in the U.S. are those of Roman Catholic, Protestant, Eastern Orthodox and Jewish faith. Sometimes couples from mixed faiths will decide to get married and have a marriage that includes components of both faiths (this is called an interfaith marriage).

It is important to note that different religions have different requirements and guidelines for a marriage ceremony. If you are planning an interfaith marriage, it will be necessary to discuss the different requirements with an officiant from each religion and determine if the two officiants will work together and how that will work.

The book *Wedding Ceremonies: Planning Your Special Day*, by Jo Packham, is a great resource to provide you with information about traditional ceremonies, customs and rituals for Roman Catholic, Protestant, Eastern Orthodox, Jewish, Mormon, Quaker, Buddhist, Muslim and interfaith wedding ceremonies. You can find a copy of this book at your local library, bookstore, or Amazon.com.

Personalizing the Ceremony and Vows

Prior to arranging a meeting with the officiant, and the bride and groom, it would be helpful to obtain a copy of the officiant's traditional ceremony script and ask them how much leeway there is to personalize the ceremony and/or vows (if this is important to your clients). If changes can be made to the ceremony and/or vows, have the bride and groom review the script and note any desired changes on a copy of the script for the initial meeting with the officiant.

If your clients want a civil or non-denominational wedding, depending on the officiant, the bride and groom are more likely to have flexibility as to what is included within the ceremony and vows. A civil wedding is a wedding that can be performed:

- At city hall by a county clerk or mayor

- By a judge in a courthouse or in the judge's chambers

- By a Justice of the Peace ("JP") at an agreed-upon location

Most JPs will allow couples to design their own ceremony or make changes to the JP's standard ceremony and add personalized vows. One thing to keep in mind is that if a non-denominational ceremony is held in a place of worship, there may be some ceremony requirements and procedures that need to be followed.

Some great resources to assist your clients with writing their own vows can be found at **http://electpress.com/loveandromance/page45.htm**. In addition to finding resources on the Internet, you may want to pick up a couple of books from the library or your local bookstore that will give you ideas on writing vows. One that will give you a number of different ideas is *Complete Book of Wedding Vows*, by Diane Warner.

For individuals getting married in the U.K., visit WeddingGuideUK.com. The following webpage not only has ideas for wedding vows but also includes the statutory words (minimum words) required to be said for the marriage to be legal there: **www.weddingguideuk.com/articles/ceremonies/vows.asp**.

As another alternative, if your clients want a unique ceremony written just for them, they should consider hiring someone to write the vows for them. The Wedding Connection can provide the service of preparing a unique ceremony, including an interfaith ceremony. Visit **www.wedconn.com/ceremonies.html** to learn more about this service. Also, try a search for freelance writers on the web or through your local telephone directory.

Exchanges and Rituals

Besides personalizing their vows, many couples like to include special exchanges and/or symbolic rituals within their ceremony.

One of the most popular exchanges is the lighting of a unity candle. The purpose of this ritual is to symbolize either the joining of the bride and groom as one, or the two families coming together in unity. This exchange often involves three candles. One is lit by either the bride (or the bride's parents) and another is lit by the groom (or the groom's parents). The bride and groom then bring the two candles together to light a center candle.

If your clients decide to perform this exchange, they will need to ensure this is acceptable to the officiant and, if so, you will need to arrange to have candles and candle holders available at the ceremony and have it included within the officiant's ceremony script.

In addition to the lighting of the unity candle, the couple may want other exchanges or rituals performed at the ceremony, such as:

- The bride takes two flowers from her bouquet, gives one to her mother and the other to the groom's mother

- An exchange of promises and/or medallions to step-children of the marriage

- Special blessings

Again, any special exchanges will need to be discussed and cleared with the officiant prior to the wedding so that they can be worked into the ceremony.

Readings and Prayers

Readings and prayers are often included in many ceremonies. Certain religions will have traditional prayers and readings that are required to be performed at all wedding ceremonies; however, sometimes there is lee-way to change the readings or add additional prayers or readings.

If your clients want to choose their own readings for their wedding, clear this with the officiant first. Your clients will then need to decide on the readings and who will perform them (sometimes the bride and/or groom will do one or more of the readings but more often they will select friends or family members to do the readings).

There are numerous resources available in print through bookstores and the library and on the Internet for help with choosing readings and prayers. You can go to your favorite search engine and type in "wedding read-ings" or "wedding prayers."

As an example, a number of readings can be found at **www.hitched. co.uk/plan/readings/index.asp**.

There are also a number of books on the subject, including *A Wedding Ceremony to Remember: Perfect Words for the Perfect Wedding*, by Marty Younkin and Carol Sage.

2.4.5 Selecting Ceremony Music

Music can be a beautiful and moving part of any wedding. Personal selections of the bride and groom can add much meaning to their ceremony. At most wedding ceremonies music is played during the following times:

- Prelude (before the wedding starts), normally commencing about 45 minutes prior to the start of the wedding as guests are arriving

- During the processional

- Intermittently throughout the ceremony (for example, when the marriage license is being signed)

- During the recessional

- After the ceremony

Various types of music and musicians can be selected for the different parts of the ceremony, including:

- Choir

- Group of musicians

- Guitar player

- Harpist

- Organist

- Pianist

- Soloist

- Pre-recorded music

Finding Musicians

To find musicians for your clients' wedding, first check with the couple to determine if they have any friends or family members who they want to perform at their ceremony.

If you are looking for an organist, pianist or choir to perform at the couple's wedding, ask at the venue if they know of any or check at your local church and see if the organist, pianist or choir there would be interested in being hired for the wedding. Musicians can also be found through local music studios where individuals are taught (look under "Music Instructors" in the Yellow Pages). If you get a lead on a good musician, ask them for a demo tape that your clients can listen to. It is important to have contracts put in place with any musicians that will be hired.

Before music selections are finalized, check with the officiant to determine if there are any rules or restrictions about what music can or cannot be played during the ceremony. In addition, you will need to find out if there are any restrictions on music being played at the venue.

Ideas for ceremony music can be found at the Ceremony Music Resource Page on the Internet at **www.intac.com/~energize/CMRP**. Music stores and larger bookstores offer a wonderful selection of compilation CDs available with a variety of beautiful music for the couple to choose from. Two that have received rave reviews are:

Bride's Guide to Wedding Music – Volume One

This CD includes mostly classical works such as:

- *A Midsummer Night's Dream* (Wedding March)
- *Canon in D* (Recessional)
- *Processional: Lohegrin* (Wedding March)
- *Spring of the Four Seasons* (Ceremony)

The Complete Wedding Album

Includes more contemporary work but also standard classics:

- *The Wedding Song*
- *Unchained Melody*
- *Love Theme from Romeo and Juliet*

These are just a few examples of what is available. It may be helpful for you to have a few on hand to help couples select their ceremony music. Once the music has been decided upon, provide each musician with a schedule confirming the date and time of the wedding and set out what music is to be played and when within the ceremony it is to be played.

2.4.6 Obtaining the Marriage License

The most important item to bring to any ceremony is the marriage license. After all, the signing of this document at a wedding ceremony is what makes the wedding legal.

Following are some general guidelines and points for your clients to consider in relation to obtaining their marriage license; however, the procedures and rules may vary from state to state.

- To determine the requirements and time needed to obtain a marriage license, contact the local marriage license bureau where the bride and groom reside and where the ceremony will be taking place. You can find the local bureau by phoning city hall and asking where marriage licenses can be obtained, or you may be able to find the marriage license bureau in your phone book in the government listings section.

  TIP: It may take up to five business days for a license to be issued, so ensure that plenty of time is given to obtain the license prior to the wedding.

- Some states require that the bride and groom obtain the license within 30 days of the wedding date, while others will allow the license to be obtained up to 90 days prior to the wedding date (although this is rare).

- Some states require each of the bride and groom to have blood tests and/or medical examinations done and to provide these records when applying for a license.

- The bride and groom should attend together at the marriage license bureau (this is a requirement in many jurisdictions) when applying for the license.

- The bride and groom should bring identification (such as a passport, birth certificate, and/or drivers' license plus they may be required to provide their social security number).

- The bride and groom should bring cash to pay the license fees.

- If the bride or groom have been married before, it would also be wise to determine if there are any rules, regulations or requirements with respect to divorcees (such as bringing a divorce decree).

As mentioned, the above points are to be used as a guideline. Your local marriage license bureau (or the bureau in the area where the ceremony will take place) will be able to provide you with the exact requirements in that particular area.

2.4.7 Ceremony Rehearsal

Besides planning, planning, and more planning, one of the best ways to ensure that the wedding ceremony will flow smoothly is to have a rehearsal in advance of the big day.

Rehearsals are normally held the afternoon or evening prior to the wedding (although they can be held even earlier than this if need be). Schedule approximately two hours for the rehearsal, which should be held at the location of the ceremony.

As the wedding planner, it is highly likely that part of your job will be to direct the rehearsal and to provide instructions to all individuals involved with the wedding ceremony (in conjunction with the officiant.) It is advisable that you contact the officiant prior to the rehearsal and determine exactly how much the officiant wants you to lead and direct the rehearsal.

Some officiants may be happy for you to take control, while others might see this as interfering with their job. If a religious ceremony has been planned, the officiant will need to provide more direction than if it is a non-denominational or civil ceremony where the couple and you have been more involved with putting together a unique ceremony.

Who Should Attend

The best plan of action is to ensure that all individuals involved with the ceremony are present at the rehearsal, including:

- The bride and groom

- The officiant

- The father (and possibly mother) of the bride

- All of the bridal attendants (including the ring-bearer and flower girl)

- Any additional ushers

- The musicians

- Anyone who is performing a reading or a prayer

- The photographer and videographer

It is a good idea to suggest to the bride and groom that when they request all participating individuals to attend the rehearsal, that they ask that the participants do not bring along any spouses, children or friends because this could cause distractions.

Prior to commencing the rehearsal:

- Have the couple provide the officiant with their marriage license to review it.

- Confirm who will be signing as witnesses on the marriage license.

- Lay out any candles that may be required for the unity candle ceremony.

- Determine the best location for the guest book.

- Handle any other last-minute details.

The rehearsal should give each member of the wedding party and all other individuals involved with the wedding an opportunity to find out their role and what is expected of them. Additionally, each person involved should be given the opportunity to practice their part and to ask any questions if they are unclear of their duties.

It is especially important for the bride and groom to practice and feel comfortable with their parts, including walking down the aisle (for the bride), passing the bouquet (for the bride), determining where they will stand, kneeling (if appropriate), signing the marriage license, exchanging vows, exchanging rings, etc.

It is ideal for you to prepare an itinerary/checklist in advance that can be handed out to all individuals involved at the rehearsal. The itinerary/checklist should include the names and duties of each person and the timing to perform each duty.

After everyone has had an opportunity to practice their parts, prior to leaving the rehearsal, it is a good idea to do a verbal run through of the ceremony and to repeat all of the instructions. Also, allow each participant the opportunity to clarify what their duties are and ask any questions if they are confused or do not understand.

In addition to providing a ceremony itinerary/checklist to all participants, a more comprehensive wedding day itinerary can also be provided to all members of the bridal party. An example of a wedding day itinerary starts on the next page.

Rehearsal Dinner

It is often customary for a rehearsal dinner or party to be held after the rehearsal. This dinner would normally include all individuals involved with the ceremony (who attended the rehearsal including the officiant) together with their partners, parents and siblings of the bride and groom, out-of-town guests and possibly the reception emcee and their partner.

It is traditional for the groom's parents to host the rehearsal dinner; however, sometimes the bride and groom themselves or other family members get involved with planning or hosting it.

Sample Wedding Day Itinerary
(for a 3:00 p.m. wedding)

In this sample itinerary it is assumed that the bride lives (or is getting ready) at a location 15 minutes away from the ceremony venue.

Time:	Action:
10:30 a.m.	Bride (and bridesmaids) attend hairdressing appointment
12:00 p.m.	Bride (and bridesmaids) have makeup done
1:00 p.m.	Bride and bridesmaids have lunch or snack (finger foods)
1:00 p.m.	Flowers are dropped off at church and final decorating is completed
1:15 p.m.	Photographer arrives at bride's location
1:15 p.m.	Bride and bridesmaids get dressed
1:30 p.m.	Flower girl and ring-bearer arrive at bride's location
1:45 p.m.	Groom and groomsmen get into formal attire
2:00 p.m.	Officiant, seating ushers and musicians arrive at ceremony venue
2:15 p.m.	Prelude music is started and guests begin to arrive
2:20 p.m.	Limousine(s) arrive at bride's location
2:30 p.m.	Groom and groomsmen arrive at ceremony venue
2:30 p.m.	Videographer arrives at ceremony venue and sets up
2:35 p.m.	First cars with mother of the bride, flower girl, ring-bearer and bridesmaids depart for ceremony venue
2:40 p.m.	Bride and father of the bride depart in limousine for the ceremony venue

2:50 p.m.	Grandmothers of the bride and groom are escorted down the aisle
2:50 p.m.	Mother of the bride, bridesmaids, flower girl and ring-bearer arrive at venue
2:52 p.m.	Mother of the groom is escorted down the aisle
2:55 p.m.	Bride and father of the bride arrive at venue
2:57 p.m.	Groom and groomsmen line up at front of venue
2:58 p.m.	Mother of the bride is escorted down the aisle
3:00 p.m.	Processional music begins and processional begins
3:45 p.m.	Ceremony ends and recessional begins
3:50 p.m.	Ceremony receiving line
4:00 p.m.	Caterer arrives at reception location
4:30 p.m.	Photographs taken at chosen location
5:30 p.m.	Cocktails and pre-recorded background music commence at reception location
6:00 p.m.	Reception receiving line with bride, groom and parents
6:30 p.m.	Reception musicians arrive and set up
6:40 p.m.	Announcement of bride and groom by emcee
6:45 p.m.	Dinner is served
7:30 p.m.	Toasts and speeches begin
7:45 p.m.	Dessert is served
8:00 p.m.	First dance of bride and groom
8:30 p.m.	Cake cutting ceremony
10:30 p.m.	Bouquet and garter toss
11:00 p.m.	Farewell dance of bride and groom
11:15 p.m.	Departure of bride and groom
12:00 a.m.	Musicians end for the evening

You may be invited to attend the rehearsal dinner as a guest. Whether you attend is optional and probably depends on your relationship with the bride and groom and how many last minute details still need to be handled. Alternatively, you may even be hired to ensure that the rehearsal party runs smoothly.

2.4.8 The Ceremony Processional, Recessional and Receiving Line

Often a wedding planner is hired to direct and oversee a wedding rehearsal and ceremony. To be able to effectively do this, you will need to know how a "typical" ceremony flows and what is involved in the processional, recessional and receiving line.

As mentioned earlier in this section of the guide, different religions have different ceremonial customs; however, many wedding ceremonies held in North America include elements of the following:

- Prelude

- Seating of the Mothers

- Processional

- Greeting

- Questions of Intent

- Readings and Music

- Wedding Vows

- Exchange of Rings

- Signing of the Marriage License

- Presentation of the Married Couple

- Recessional

Processional

Non-Denominational or Standard Christian

An example of a typical non-denominational ceremony processional (which is also reflective of a standard Christian processional) is set out below in the order of occurrence. Again, depending on the specific religion, the officiant and/or the desires of the bride and groom, there could be variances to this standard.

1. Immediately before the processional starts, the mother of the bride is escorted to her seat by one of the ushers.

2. The groom, best man and groomsmen enter through a side door and take their place at the altar (or at the front), facing the guests.

   OR:

   Processional music begins. The groomsmen and best man walk down the aisle (they can either go in single-file or in pairs) followed by the groom.

3. The bridesmaids walk down the aisle (either in single-file or in pairs).

4. The maid of honor walks down the aisle.

5. The ring-bearer walks down the aisle.

6. The flower girl walks down the aisle (sometimes she walks together with the ring-bearer).

7. Wedding March (bridal entrance music) begins and guests stand up.

8. The bride and her father (or other escort) walk down the aisle. The guests sit down at the direction of the officiant

After the bride arrives at the front she will let go of her father (sometimes there is a giving away of the bride by the father and often he will kiss the bride before seating himself beside his wife). The bride will then stand beside the groom and either hold his hand or link her right arm around the groom's left arm.

Or, in a Roman Catholic wedding, the father will escort the bride to the altar where the groom and priest are situated, place her hand in the groom's hand and then the father will lift the bride's veil and kiss her before he seats himself beside his wife (the bride is not given away in a Catholic ceremony).

Arrangement at Front

In most cases, the officiant will be at the front facing the guests and the bride and groom and all other members of the bridal party will be facing the officiant with the bride and her attendants (including the flower girl) on the left and the groom and his attendants (including the ring-bearer) on the right.

Normally the maid of honor, with the flower girl beside her, will stand directly to the left of the bride. The other bridesmaids stand beside the flower girl. The same line-up is used for the groom and his party, with the ring-bearer standing beside the best man, who is directly to the right of the groom. The other groomsmen stand beside the ring-bearer. Although this is the standard way the bridal party is lined up, there are no rules dictating this arrangement.

> **TIP:** It will help to have all members of the bridal party practice the processional and lining up at the altar (or front) at the rehearsal held prior to the wedding. To assist the members of the bridal party so that they know how much distance to give each other when standing up front, you may want to lay a rose petal where each person is supposed to stand.

Jewish Processionals

Jewish ceremony processionals are somewhat different and involve certain rituals which can vary according to the Jewish observances.

It is somewhat typical to have a Jewish processional with the rabbi walking down the aisle first, followed by the groomsmen in single-file, then best man, the groom escorted by both his parents (with his father on his left and his mother on his right), the bridesmaids in single-file, the maid of honor, the ring-bearer and flower girl and finally the bride escorted by her parents (with her father on her left and her mother on her right). Sometimes the grandparents are even part of the processional.

There are certain rituals involved in a Jewish ceremony processional. For example, a Ketuba (a marriage document written in Aramaic) needs to be delivered by the groom, plus an article of value is presented by the groom to the bride (often a gold ring), there is the veiling of the bride by the groom prior to the ceremony beginning, etc.

Once the bride and groom arrive at the front of the synagogue (after the processional), they will stand with the rabbi under a chuppah (canopy). The bride stands on the right side with her maid of honor standing to the right of her. The bride's parents and other attendants then stand beside them. The groom stands to the left side, with the best man standing to the left of him. His parents and other attendants stand beside them.

There are many other rituals and customs that need to be understood and followed, so if you will be involved with co-ordinating a Jewish wedding, you should not only attend some Jewish weddings to watch how they flow but you should also meet with the rabbi and ask about the customs and read as many books as possible to ensure that you fully understand what is required.

To find out more information about ceremony processionals, recessionals and receiving lines for other religions, you can refer to the book previously mentioned titled *Wedding Ceremonies: Planning Your Special Day*, by Jo Packham.

Recessional

The recessional occurs after the ceremony ends. An example of a typical non-denominational (or standard Christian) ceremony recessional follows.

1. Recessional music begins (usually upbeat and uplifting music)

2. The bride and groom walk arm in arm down the aisle.

3. The ring-bearer and flower girl walk together down the aisle.

4. The maid of honor and the best man walk arm in arm down the aisle.

5. The remaining bridesmaids and groomsmen pair off (one bridesmaid with one groomsman) and walk arm in arm down the aisle.

6. The officiant walks down the aisle.

7. The bride's parents walk down the aisle.

8. The groom's parents walk down the aisle.

9. The groomsmen return to escort guests out.

Receiving Line

As soon as the ceremony is over, the guests will want an opportunity to go up and congratulate the bride and groom. Most guests are excited to share in the wedding day and want to be able to express this to the couple (and often to their parents). Although it is not always done, it is a nice touch to arrange a receiving line so that guests can greet the bride and groom together.

As the wedding planner, you may need to round up the bride and groom and their parents and line them up at the back of the venue (or the vestibule of the church, if permitted) because with the excitement of the moment, this could easily be forgotten.

It is a good idea to discuss the receiving line, and who will be involved and where it will occur, at the rehearsal the day before the wedding so that there are no surprises and everyone involved knows what to expect.

If the couple prefers, you can arrange to have a receiving line at the reception.

2.4.9 Other Ceremony Arrangements

In addition to all of the ceremony planning information provided above, it is also helpful to know about the other arrangements you may be involved in co-ordinating as a wedding planner. These could include ordering invitations and flowers, arranging transportation, and co-ordinating with the photographer and videographer.

For detailed information about working with vendors who will supply these services, see section 2.6 of this guide.

2.5 Planning the Reception

As important as the wedding ceremony is, the event that will take the most planning time and eat up most of the budget is the reception.

Types of Receptions

There are no hard and fast rules for what constitutes a reception. While most wedding receptions have at least three of the following elements, your clients should be reassured that the elimination of one or more of these elements will not ruin their memories of the day or have their guests gossiping for years to come:

- Food

- Drink

- Dancing

- Speeches

- Traditional rituals (bouquet toss, cake cutting, etc.)

- Receiving line or introductions

There are almost as many possible variations on the above as there are brides. Here are some examples:

- Early morning ceremony followed by a mid-morning brunch and speeches (no dance or liquor)

- Mid-morning ceremony followed by a late afternoon lunch (no dance or liquor)

- Family-only wedding dinner followed by a candlelight ceremony and a dance

- Afternoon ceremony, followed by a family-only dinner, guest dessert buffet and dance

- Afternoon ceremony followed by a dinner and gift opening (no dance or liquor)

- Late afternoon ceremony followed by a cocktail reception (no dance or formal dinner)

- Evening candlelight ceremony followed by a dance and hors d'oeuvres and dessert

Regardless of the type of reception your clients would like, you will still have to find and book a venue and probably arrange for some type of catered food.

It would be impossible for us to tell you, in the space of this book alone, how to plan every single detail of each possible type of wedding and reception. What we will provide is a general overview of what goes into planning the average reception and let your creativity and imagination go from here.

2.5.1 Venue Selection

Choosing an appropriate venue for the reception is vitally important to the success of the event. On top of the wishes of your clients, some of the many things that should be taken into consideration include:

- **Capacity:** Will the room hold the required number of people comfortably?

- **Cleanliness:** Is the venue clean and in good repair?

- **Suitability:** Is it suitable for a catered affair or used mainly for meetings?

- **Grounds:** Is there a view or nicely landscaped grounds for guests to enjoy, or for wedding party photos?

- **Dance Floor:** Is the space the appropriate size for the number of people?

- **Kitchen Facilities:** Extremely important if venue is a community hall and the caterer is expected to serve and cook on-site — does the venue have refrigeration and heating appliances? Dishes and cutlery?

- **Washroom Facilities:** Are handicapped facilities available? Can a bride fit into a stall wearing a wedding dress? Are they clean?

- **Audio/Visual:** Are there enough outlets for the A/V requirements? Does the venue provide a microphone?

- **Lighting:** Can the lights be dimmed for the dance or presentations? Is there enough lighting for food service and speeches?

- **Seating:** Are the chairs clean and comfortable? Are there extra chairs?

- **Linens:** Does the venue supply linens, including draping for tables?

- **Stage or Platform:** Does the venue supply any of these items for use by a band, DJ and/or emcee?

- **Electrical:** Is the power supply sufficient for a band and/or DJ's needs?

- **Tables:** How many tables are there, and what configurations are available? Are there extra tables?

- **Bar:** Is the bar portable or static? Is it stocked with openers, glasses and an icemaker or refrigerator?

- **Cleanup:** Does the venue provide janitorial service and garbage disposal?

- **On-site Co-ordination:** Does the venue have its own event co-ordinator? If so, what is their role?

One of the best ways for you to check out a venue in your area is to conduct a site survey. A site survey (or inspection) is a visit to a venue to learn as much as possible about its facilities.

You conduct a site survey by calling ahead to arrange an appointment with the person who is in charge of renting the space, or their delegate. This could be the facility manager, events co-ordinator, or catering manager. When you call to arrange the inspection make sure you get the contact's name, correct address and any driving instructions that may be needed. Tell them you are a wedding planner and would like to visit their facility when it is unoccupied and you are free to wander extensively.

Beware if the person on the phone tries to convince you not to visit and would rather just send you a brochure. Most reputable facilities will have marketing materials (brochures and such) on hand that they are more than happy to give you; however, the best opinion on what a facility is really like is yours. Have you ever booked a hotel room by simply seeing a brochure, only to find out that what looked like 1000 square feet turns out to be more like 100? A good photographer is like a magician and can make the smallest room seem like a palace.

Before you make your first appointment, design a simple facility survey sheet that you can later refer to as a reminder of what you saw and, perhaps more importantly, didn't see. Include the name and address of the venue, the contact's name and phone number and an after hours contact name and number.

On this sheet you can note the items listed above, plus any other observations — from the staff's attitude to the décor (or lack thereof). Your survey sheet could look something like the one on pages 90-91.

Add a large blank space for notes and comments. Your reputation as a professional is on the line here so take copious detailed notes. If you are not comfortable doing this during the site survey, take a few minutes to jot down your impressions as soon as you get in your car and before you drive to your next appointment.

Typical comments could be:

- "Great summer venue but not suitable for winter weddings"

- "No handicapped facilities and difficult to get to"

- "Floors and carpets need to be replaced and walls are dingy"

Sample Reception Site Survey Sheet

General Information

Venue: _____

Address: _____
_____

Website: _____
Contact name: _____
Title: _____
Phone: _____
Fax: _____
E-mail: _____

Venue Information

Rooms

Seating capacity: _____
Number of rooms: _____
Floor plans available: Y / N
Outdoor facilities available: Y / N
Describe outdoor facilities here:
_____
_____

Food Service

On-site catering: Y / N
Staff: _____
Kitchen: _____
Bar: _____

Dining/Decorating

Linens: _____
Table decorations: _____
Allow candles: Y / N
Describe any available natural/artificial lighting here:
_____
_____

Audio/Visual Capabilities

Describe the venue's audio/visual capabilities here:

_____

_____

Parking

Number of parking spaces: _____

Charge per space: _____

Washrooms

Number of washrooms: _____

Describe the overall condition here:

_____

_____

Handicapped Facilities

Washrooms: _____

Parking: _____

Ramps: _____

Cleanliness

Janitorial service included: Y / N

Describe the overall cleanliness here:

_____

_____

Fees and Policies

Gratuities: _____

Deposit: _____

Cancellation policy:

_____

_____

Comments

Include personal notes and comments here:

_____

_____

2.5.2 Preparing for the Reception

Once the venue has been chosen, your role may include negotiating the contract, as well as supervising all arrangements for the reception. Section 2.6 of this guide (Working with Vendors) has more information about the contract and follow-up involved with all vendors. This section covers information specific to working with venues.

Trust the Experts

If your clients decide to hold their reception in a hotel function room or venue such as a private room in a restaurant, country club or other wedding site (like a pavilion), most of the room setup and catering will be professionally handled by an on-staff event co-ordinator. You will still assist in choosing the menu and program for the evening but you will act as liaison between the venue co-ordinator and your client.

In addition to conferring with the site's event co-ordinator, you might also be introduced to the venue's wine steward and catering manager to assist in planning any food service requirements. For the most part you will find these people to be friendly, professional and extremely helpful. Trust their judgment on items pertaining to the space and allow them to assist in choosing appropriate wine and food pairings. They are experts in these matters and have done dozens, if not hundreds, of weddings before.

As mentioned in section 2.6 of this guide (Working with Vendors), treat these individuals and all of their staff with kindness and respect and they will go above and beyond what is normally expected to ensure the success of your event. Do not be afraid to ask them for help or for another opinion if necessary.

Planning a reception at one of these venues is made easy by the expert advice you receive. So, what happens if your clients choose an out of the ordinary venue or a community center that has not been set up for this type of function? Simple. Trust the experts! The experts in this case will be independent caterers, the staff at the venue, and musicians who also have experience in handling and setting up weddings.

We believe there are solutions for every unusual circumstance and problem and asking for advice is the best way to learn. Here are a couple of examples of weddings planned by one of the authors of this guide:

Wedding in a Remote Location

Our clients hoped for an outdoor wedding on a piece of property owned by a relative. The area chosen for the ceremony and reception was isolated from standard kitchen facilities and power. The solution: we chose a catering company that was set up to cater to remote movie locations.

The menu consisted of a hip of beef that was barbecued in huge outdoor ovens towed in on a trailer and the rest of the meal was prepared in the huge motorhome-style truck. The caterer provided wait staff, table linens, plates, and cutlery. The entire food preparation area was hidden behind curtained-off areas. Everything else was rented and delivered to the site by the rental company. This included tables, chairs, tents, flooring material, and some decorations. Portable generators supplied the power and outdoor washroom facilities were rented. Transportation to ferry guests to the site was provided by a chartered bus company.

Beach Wedding

Another couple wanted to get married on the beach in front of their property but not to use their small home for guests or caterers. The ceremony was to be held on a small pier on the waterfront with a party on the beach to follow immediately after. An inexperienced caterer and wedding planner would run in horror from this situation but the company chosen had done many luau-style events and was up for the challenge.

A whole pig was roasted, and shellfish (shrimp, mussels and oysters) and a variety of cold salads were served to the guests from small wooden canoes on stands filled with crushed ice. Umbrellas were everywhere to give respite from the afternoon sun. The only hot food was the pork and everything else was kept cool in the refrigerated compartment of the caterer's van until ready to serve. Music was provided by a sound system in the home to speakers set up on the beach, and of course everything else was rented.

The old saying "where there's a will there's a way" should become every wedding planner's motto.

If the venue is a hall and the caterer is bringing or preparing the food on-site, ask for their advice. Caterers can provide uniformed wait staff, bartenders, and nearly every piece of equipment necessary for the preparation and serving of the meal. You can also enlist the help of the caterers to rent all of the other items not associated with the meal, but you will pay a small premium to have them arrange for rental and transport of these items.

Rental companies will also provide almost everything you can think of for a wedding. Some of the items you may rent from a rental company are: dishes, linens, wine and drink glasses, cutlery, tables, chairs, tents, coat racks, BBQs, cooking equipment, chafing dishes, table decorations, archways, helium tanks for balloons, carpet runners, bartending equipment, garbage containers, large coffee makers, portable washroom facilities, etc.

Reviewing the Contract

Before your clients sign the contract for the venue check it over very carefully and be aware of the following items:

- What time the venue is available for decorating or suppliers delivering goods. Will the facility be open, or are there instructions on how to get the key?

- How many hours the rental period covers. Is there an hourly charge for overages?

- Cancellation policy

- Clean up/tear down requirements

- Total cost, deposit schedule and final payment dates

- How damages are handled and if an inspection is carried out prior to and following your event

- 24-hour contact number for emergencies

Room Layout

Once again, the venue co-ordinator will be very helpful in designing a room layout that is both functional and stylish. If the wedding is to be held in a hall that does not have an event co-ordinator, keep the following points in mind:

- Optimally, the room should be large enough to accommodate a dance floor without having to remove tables and other furnishings.

- There should always be a clear pathway to washrooms, the bar area, kitchen area and the dance floor.

- You will most likely require a table close to the entrance for guest book signing.

- The cake table should be situated away from traffic paths and also in a nicely decorated area where photographs will be taken.

- If the meal is to be buffet style try to design the room layout with both sides of the tables easily accessed. This will shorten lineups and thus wait time.

- Try to arrange seating so everyone has an unobstructed view of the head table. If the room has pillars or other obstructions, try not to place tables behind them.

- Provide a gift table.

- If the wedding is during the winter or fall months, ensure there are adequate coat check facilities or provide rented coat racks and place in an inconspicuous area.

Food and Beverage Selection

The bride and groom and their respective families may want you to help them select the menu for the dinner (or other meal) and accompanying wine or champagne choices.

If you have not taken wine and food pairing courses or are not an accomplished chef or caterer it would be wise of you to state this up front and trust the advice of the professionals. You should certainly feel free to offer suggestions using ideas from previous weddings you've planned, but other than that it is usually wise to stay within your realm of expertise.

Couples today are more aware of the dietary requirements of their guests and are likely to request kosher, vegetarian, low-fat or other special diet considerations when planning the meal. One way to glean this information from the guests is to add a line to the RSVP card where guests can make their dietary concerns known. Keep a list of those individuals who request a special meal and make sure it is given to the caterer well in advance of the wedding.

Consideration should also be given to children's meals (if there will be children attending) and for those who choose not to consume alcohol. Providing non-alcoholic drinks (such as sparkling non-alcoholic beverages) for the toast and dinner, will be appreciated by those guests who choose not to drink alcohol.

A liquor merchant or liquor representative will be an invaluable resource for those weddings that are held in community centers or other facilities that do not have on-staff caterers and event co-ordinators.

Before meeting with prospective caterers, ask your clients the following questions:

- If the reception follows a morning ceremony will the meal be a brunch or lunch?

- What type of service would they prefer: a formal sit-down dinner or a buffet? If a buffet is chosen, will the head table be served?

- Will hors d'oeuvres be served prior to the dinner?

- Will the food requirements include a late evening light meal or snack?

- Are there cultural or other ethnic food restrictions that need to be considered when booking a caterer?

- Will the wedding cake be used as the dessert course or will a separate dessert be required?

- How many courses would they prefer? (A standard sit-down meal usually consists of a soup/salad course, main entrée and dessert courses. This will vary depending on cultural background and budget. For instance, Italian weddings generally include a pasta course, fish course, and entrée on top of a soup/salad and dessert course!)

Decorating the Reception Venue

Decorations have come a long way since the early days of wedding bell crepe paper cutouts, streamers and balloons. With the trend toward themed weddings, decorating the reception venue has become more challenging but a great opportunity to show off your creative side.

Even if the reception venue is a country club or hotel ballroom and the tables are normally beautifully decorated, every bride will want to add special touches, colors and flowers that co-ordinate with her chosen colors or theme.

Think outside the box when brainstorming for decorating ideas. Ask the couple plenty of lifestyle questions when attempting to come up with a unique theme. For instance, if the couple tells you they are avid sailors, a nautical theme may be appropriate. Here are some other ideas:

- Centerpieces can be mini-sailboats filled with fresh fruit or flowers. Flowers as centerpieces may be eliminated altogether in favor of fresh flower petals strewn artfully across the entire table.

- Don't overlook chairs when decorating tables. Linen rental companies can supply lovely fabric chair drapes which you can then tuck an appropriately chosen flower into the sash on the back of the chair to add a touch of elegance.

- Lighting is often overlooked when decorating the reception venue. Candles offer a soft hue which adds ambiance to the dullest space. If candles are not permitted try using mini-string lights wound through artificial trees, plants or other greenery.

- Archways are always popular and can provide a wonderful backdrop for taking pictures during the cake cutting ceremony.

Many of the resources we've mentioned throughout this guide can be useful places to get ideas from other brides and planners, but other helpful places for decorating ideas include bridal and fashion magazines such as *Martha Stewart Living*, home decorating books or magazines like *Style at Home* or *AmericanStyle*. There are countless books available on everything from table setting to room décor.

Typically the venue will be decorated the day of the wedding but there may be exceptions to this if there is no function booked in the room the evening before. It doesn't hurt to ask if you can get access to the venue earlier. Be aware there may be an extra charge for gaining early access, and make sure this is covered in the budget if that is the case.

Thank-You Novelties

In years gone by the standard token of appreciation by the bride and groom to their guests included a very small piece of wedding cake wrapped in a paper doily with a little thank-you note attached. These were either handed out to each guest as the couple made the rounds at the reception, or left on a table for guests to help themselves.

Over the years variations on this theme emerged which included mints wrapped in tulle or small boxes of chocolates. These were set at each place setting and either taken home or eaten at the dinner. Today the variety of token gifts is limited only by imagination and can include (to name just a few):

- Mini flower pots and seeds

- Individual tea light candles

- A silk flower at each place

- Miniature picture frames complete with a picture of the couple (an engagement photo, perhaps)

Craft stores are wonderful places to start the imaginative juices flowing, as are the many websites dedicated to all things bridal. One of the largest craft supply stores in North America is Michaels. If you have access to the Internet, check out **www.michaels.com** to find a store near you.

2.5.3   Reception Activities

Receiving Line

For a standard size wedding (100-150 people) you should allow approximately 30-45 minutes for everyone to make it through the receiving line. As mentioned in the previous section, couples may choose to have the receiving line after the ceremony, and in this case the reception receiving line should be eliminated. If held before the reception, the wedding party should arrive just slightly ahead of the guests, or soon after.

There are many definitions of family, and with ever-increasing divorce rates and blending of families, some couples are choosing to forego a traditional receiving line in favor of bridal party introductions. Here is how one of the authors of this guide planned this for one recently wed couple:

> While the bridal party was off having their photographs taken, we were in contact with the father of the bride via cell phone. When the photographer was done and the couple was on their way to the reception venue, we had the Master of Ceremonies ask everyone to be seated for dinner. We then ushered the wedding party into the reception area while the Master of Ceremonies introduced them to the guests. The last couple to enter the room, to rousing applause, was the bride and groom. They were seated at the head table and the dinner began.

Speeches

Speeches are traditionally made after dinner when coffee, tea and dessert have been served. They can be eloquent formal speeches, heartfelt casual wishes, or anything in between. Couples often opt to offer a toast to their wedding party together. Also, they will not only have a close friend or relative offer a toast to the bride, but a person from the groom's side will do the same for him.

Your clients will handle selection of the individuals who will act as Master of Ceremonies and offer the toast to the bride (and possibly groom). If the people giving toasts need advice, there are a variety of websites offering wedding speeches and toasts. If they would prefer to purchase a book, there are many choices. One that's filled with great advice is *The Complete Book of Wedding Toasts*, by John William McCluskey.

A speech may also be supplemented with a video montage or other type of visual or audio presentation, and some couples provide a short time during the speeches for their guests to tell little stories, share memories or pass on good wishes during an open microphone opportunity. You should be aware of the possibility of this so as to be prepared with the appropriate audio/visual equipment and power source. The speeches will take approximately 45 minutes to one hour to complete.

Dance

The venue co-ordinator is the best person to ask about where the musicians or DJ should be situated. If the reception is being held in a hall without a co-ordinator, ask the DJ or bandleader to meet with you to determine their needs and arrange a setup time. DJs and musicians may want to do a partial setup and sound check prior to the guests arriving. They will complete their setup immediately following the speeches.

If the clients so desire, the dancing may begin with a waltz for the bridal couple only, followed by dances by father-daughter, mother-son, the wedding party and other relatives. While the above list is a fairly traditional representation there are many variations on this depending on dynamics of the family, ethnic practices, etc.

Your job will be to gather together the couple, their bridal party and any other combination of people they request to the dance floor for the dance to begin.

Bouquet and Garter Toss

You will advise the DJ or musicians when it is time to announce the bouquet and garter toss. It's your job to ensure the selected flowers or special bouquet is ready for the bride to throw.

The single wedding guests are called to the dance floor. Then the bouquet is tossed to the female guests and then the garter (if worn) is tossed to the male guests. Be sure to ask the couple if they want this tradition included in the festivities. Remember, everyone is not of the same background and beliefs, and this activity may be frowned upon.

Cake Cutting Ceremony

On your cue, the DJ or musicians will announce the cake cutting ceremony. Some couples serve their wedding cake as dessert. If this is the case, the cake cutting ceremony will, of course, take place immediately following dinner and before the speeches begin.

The cake cutting ceremony is one of the photo opportunities that occur at the reception. The announcement should be made prior to the couple making their way to the cake table to give the guests time to gather up their cameras and position themselves. Give the bridal couple plenty of notice that this is about to happen so they can make a quick run to the powder room to freshen up.

You are responsible for ensuring that the cake table is prepared and ready for the ceremony. If the venue does not have a co-ordinator, position the cake table well out of a main traffic path.

The cake table is another area that can reflect your creative decorating touch while maintaining continuity with the wedding theme or colors. You can add flowers, lighting, candles and other decorations.

Put the cake cutting knife on your list of items to look after and ensure it is placed on the table prior to the ceremony. You may want to keep the knife out of sight until the ceremony begins to ensure the safety of the little fingers of those children attending.

Evening Light Meal

As awareness of the consequences of drinking and driving increases, many couples simply choose to serve their guests a light meal about mid-way through the dance. Many choices are available and can include a simple buffet of cold cuts, or hot and cold hors d'oeuvres, buns, assorted cheeses, squares or wedding cake and coffee.

The budget will, to a great extent, dictate the quantity and type of meal (sometimes called "late lunch") served. Caterers will offer a variety of suggestions to suit every budget so make sure you know what the budgeted amount is well in advance of the meeting with the caterer to make choosing the menu easier.

Distribute Vendor Payments

Not all wedding planners will get involved in the disbursement of checks to the vendors. If you decide to offer this service, you will be responsible for ensuring the caterer, DJ or musicians, bartender, wait staff, clean up crew, and any other vendors are paid at the end of the evening. Carry a briefcase or file with these payments (preferably sealed in envelopes) inside and try to find a secure location at the venue to store them until the end of the evening.

Tear Down and Clean Up

While not customary, you may be asked to supervise tear down and clean up of the facilities. Items that have been rented should be returned to the containers they came in for next day pickup or put into storage for next day drop-off.

Most rental companies do not expect their dishes and glasses to be washed or their linens cleaned. This is included in the rental prices. Food items are scraped off the plates and they are returned to the containers that were provided for this purpose.

2.6 Working with Vendors

Vendors (also known as "*suppliers*") are sellers of merchandise or services that may be used before, during or after a wedding. Following is a list of typical vendors involved with a wedding. It is by no means complete, but it will give you a good idea of how many different individuals and businesses are involved in the successful planning of a wedding:

- Bakers

- Bridal shops

- Calligraphers

- Caterers

- Ceremony venues

- Confectioners

- Decorators

- Disc jockeys (DJs)

- Florists

- Jewellers

- Limousine rentals

- Linen suppliers

- Musicians

- Party supply rentals

- Photographers

- Printers

- Reception venues

- Stationers

- Travel agents

- Tuxedo rentals

- Videographers

It is not necessary for you to understand every facet of each vendor's particular business because your role will be as a liaison between your client and the vendor. With some exceptions, depending on the type of service or product, your job will be the same with the different vendors.

You may do any or all of the following:

- Recommend vendors

- Meet with the vendors chosen by your clients

- Review and negotiate vendor contracts

- Prepare a letter of understanding

- Wedding day co-ordination and supervision

- Follow-up after the wedding

2.6.1 Recommending Vendors

While a few couples may know all the vendors they want to work with, many clients will ask you to recommend vendors. Since you may need to do this on short notice, it's a good idea to do your homework ahead of time, and have a list of "preferred vendors" ready when clients ask.

So how do you find vendors to recommend to clients? If you begin your career as a wedding planner by working for a vendor such as a bridal shop or caterer, you will have a good starting place. The people you work with can become resources for you to call upon later.

But how do you get to know vendors when you are the new kid on the block or have not yet met anyone from these industries? Fortunately, there are a variety of ways to find vendors. Start by asking friends or family members who have recently been married in your area about the vendors they used and whether they were happy with the services of those vendors.

Next, look for vendors that advertise their services for weddings. For example, although you can check the Yellow Pages by type of vendor (such as "Florist") to find those that specialize in weddings, also try looking under "Wedding Suppliers" or "Wedding Services."

You can also find these vendors by attending bridal shows (see section 5.3.5) or by adding the word "wedding" if you are doing an online search.

Arrange a Meeting

However, before you can recommend vendors to your clients, you will need to check them out. One of the best ways for you to educate yourself about vendors in your area is to meet with them in person. Simply phone and ask to arrange an appointment with the owner or manager. Explain that you are a wedding planner, and are looking for vendors to recommend to your clients.

Any vendor that wants more business should be happy to meet with you. If they say they are busy and want to send you information, you can certainly look at what they send. However, it is wise to meet with anyone you might be working with before recommending them to a client.

Depending on the type of vendor, they may be able to show you photo albums, or a "portfolio" with samples of their work. For example, when you meet with a photographer, you can look through albums that include wedding photos and notice the quality of the pictures taken and if the photos capture the romance of the day.

Also, find out if the photographer takes candid photos as well as posed photos. Often the candid photos are the ones that capture the moment best and may be the photos that your clients will be most thrilled to have.

Remember that the vendors are experts in their areas. Most should be able to offer a variety of ideas and options for your clients. For example, florists that service weddings will have photo albums or picture books that show examples of bouquets and other wedding floral arrangements so that the bride and groom can get ideas for ordering.

In addition to viewing any samples, your meeting will give you an opportunity to find out what wedding day packages the vendor offers and what is included.

Questions to Ask

To ensure you get all the information you need from your meeting, it's a good idea to come prepared with a list of specific questions to ask. You can either take notes on a notepad or design a "survey sheet" for each type of vendor you meet with. (A sample survey sheet for checking out a venue appears in section 2.5.1.)

The particular questions you use for a visit to a retailer, wholesaler or supplier will be tailored to the specific services they provide. For instance, you can ask a DJ for a playlist (a list or inventory of the songs they have) or ask a florist if they deliver all table and church arrangements and set them up. To illustrate what you might ask, here are some questions you could ask a videographer:

- How many hours will the videographer work (will they record both the ceremony and the reception) and what is the cost?

- Will the videographer attend the rehearsal (what is the cost for this)?

- How much deposit is required and when is it payable?

- When is the final payment due?

- What is the cancellation policy?

- What are the overtime costs?

- How many cameras will be used?

- Will cordless microphones be used?

- Will the video be edited?

- Will any special effects be added (e.g. fading in or out)?

- Will music be added to the video?

- Does the package price include a certain number of DVDs or tapes?

- How much will it cost for additional DVDs or tapes?

- Are there any other costs?

- How long after the wedding will the video be available?

You can find other examples of questions to ask vendors in section 2.4 of this guide. The following websites also offer very good advice on how to select a vendor and questions to ask when determining if a vendor would be right for your client. While written specifically for brides, the information is easily adapted for use by wedding planners.

- *Getting the Most From Your Wedding Service Provider* **www.bridestuff.com/articles/providerscl.asp**

- *American Bridal Accessories – Planning Checklist* **www.americanbridal.com/planchec.html**

If you are computer savvy you could build a database of suppliers and include your observations on each survey in a file stored on your computer. If you are not comfortable using a database program you could just as easily slip your survey sheets into a three-ring binder with the sheets inserted first by type of service and then alphabetically, or whatever method works best for you.

Choosing Reputable Vendors

Perhaps the most important piece of advice we can give you about selecting vendors is to choose those who have a good reputation in the community and a great service record. As the wedding planner, your own reputation depends on the success or failure of vendor services. It may seem unfair, but if the wedding cake doesn't arrive on time and the limo gets lost and the photographer shows up drunk, people will remember YOUR name!

Before adding a business to your preferred vendors list, ask for references from previous clients. Call those references to find out what services the vendor provided, and whether the clients were satisfied. To uncover any problems, ask the client what they would do differently if they were hiring the same vendor, and which parts of the vendor's services they were least satisfied with.

Even if all the references are positive, it's wise to contact your local Better Business Bureau to see if they have any complaints on file about the vendor. To locate a BBB anywhere in the U.S. or Canada, visit their website at **www.bbb.org**.

Once you've done a number of weddings you will know which vendors deliver what they promise and you will have built a preferred list of vendors you can recommend.

> **TIP:** Some vendors may offer you a "kickback" for any business you refer to them. For example, if your client spends $1,000 with the vendor, the vendor would pay you $100. Although most wedding planners pass on any price reduction to the client, some wedding planners keep the kickback. It's not illegal to do so, but recommending a vendor just because they give you a kickback can cost you a lot more in the long run if they don't do a good job for your clients.

Meeting with the Chosen Vendor

Once you've built a list of preferred vendors you will help your clients choose a vendor that suits their budget and preferences. Of course, the client may decide to use a vendor that a friend or relative has recommended and this should not pose a problem for you. In fact, it could be a good opportunity for you to get to know the service and reliability of another vendor.

If you have had dealings with that particular vendor and the service or quality has been substandard, you should inform your clients but in the end allow them to decide.

While some of your clients may be comfortable visiting the vendors alone to choose their own wedding supplies (cakes, flowers, decorations, etc.), you should be prepared for those clients that want you to go with them to assist in making selections. (If you are providing complete wedding planning services, this will be part of the services you provide.)

2.6.2 Contract Negotiation

Most wedding professionals list their powers of negotiation with vendors (their cost savings potential) as a key reason why a client should consider hiring them. The better negotiator you are, the lower your client's costs will be.

> **TIP:** Most vendors expect you to negotiate, and many will give you a "corporate rate" or subtract 10% from the price simply because you ask for a discount.

The optimal result of any negotiation is to come away in a win-win situation for everyone. As you become more experienced and known in the wedding industry it will become easier for you to negotiate deals with vendors because of the volume of work you can bring them. Until you earn a reputation in the industry you will have to be a little more creative to negotiate the best possible prices for your clients. Here are some effective negotiating tips.

Negotiate with the Right Person

Do not waste your time negotiating with people who do not have the authority to give you a discount. You may get along really well with a venue sales co-ordinator but if the general manager is the only person with the authority to make deals, then go directly to them.

Be Prepared

A vital part of negotiating is knowledge. If you enter into a negotiation about the price for a service without first finding out the industry average you will not know if the price the vendor is suggesting is fair or not. Do your homework and gather information on pricing and other variables from as many vendors as possible.

Be Creative

If a vendor won't budge on the issue of price, try to get them to include something that won't cost them much, but will give the client perceived value. For instance:

> The florist you are negotiating with will not move on the price for the bride's bouquet. You feel the price is unreasonable but know how popular this particular shop is with brides. Perhaps you could get them to throw in a bunch of greenery that you could use for decorating the archway. The florist gets their greenery for very little cost and is happy to comply. You were going to buy artificial greenery for the archway but can now use fresh, and the bride is very happy as she gets free archway decoration. Everybody wins in this situation.

Here are just a few examples of items you can negotiate a lower price on or try to get for free:

- Price of reception room if a certain number of guest bedrooms are booked through a hotel

- Free parking with a venue that normally charges a fee

- A limited number of free bottles of champagne if total liquor package is ordered through one vendor

- Reduction in price for a guarantee of a "block booking" (booking a certain number of guest bedrooms) at a hotel

- Free flower girl basket if all other flowers ordered through one florist

- Free wedding cake by a caterer if a number of different events are also booked through the same caterer (e.g. rehearsal dinner, bridesmaids luncheon, and reception)

- Hospitality room used as a dressing room for the bridal party if hotel is used for other functions (i.e. reception room, guest bedrooms, ceremony location)

Come Ready to Deal

When entering a negotiation phase with a vendor, be prepared to offer something in return. If the vendor is relatively new to the marketplace and trying to build a client base, you could offer to pass out their business cards at your next networking opportunity or to partner with them at a bridal show. Come up with a list of ways your service is unique and can benefit theirs and be ready to use the list at the negotiating table. If you are working with clients who are influential people in your city, make sure the vendor knows this.

Use Smart Negotiating Tactics

One of the best ways of ensuring you are getting a good deal from a vendor is to tell them you are shopping around and getting comparative bids from their competitors.

Another tactic often used is the offer of an immediate deal if the vendor reduces their price by a certain percentage. The vendor may be willing to give the discount rather than have you leave the premises to shop around.

Finally, don't be afraid to ask for what you want. The worst that can happen is that someone refuses. After all, if you are persistent and ask for three things, the vendor might just give you one and you walk away with one more thing than you started with!

Reviewing the Contract

Once you have reached an agreement with the vendor, you should review the vendor contract with your clients to ensure they fully understand what they are signing. There should always be a contract in place and even if it is a very simple one it should be carefully reviewed. Some of the important information to note is:

Cost

Is the vendor charging a fair price for the service, and is the price the same as the one negotiated? Before your client signs, check to ensure the vendor has not added any unnecessary items or services.

Cancellation Policy

This is very important for your clients to know. Most engaged couples have the expectation that their wedding will go off as planned; however, in the real world people have been known to call off weddings months before the date and even at the last minute. For that reason, every client should have a clear understanding of the vendor's cancellation policy.

Service Provided

Every contract should accurately detail exactly what (and more importantly what will not) be provided. For example, if the vendor is a caterer and the venue is a community hall it is important to know if the caterer will provide wait staff, linens, dishes, bar and wine glasses, and setup/cleanup staff.

> **TIP:** Make sure the contract is between the vendor and your clients, NOT between the vendor and you. If you enter into a contract with a vendor, you will be held personally liable for payment if the wedding is cancelled or postponed.

2.6.3 Co-ordination with the Vendor

After the contract has been signed and delivered, you are responsible for contacting the vendor to arrange the logistics.

It is important to learn about vendors' timelines and scheduling. You will also need to know whether they deliver and set up, or whether they require you to pick up items from them. Ultimately, you will be responsible for seeing that all of these items come together on time for the wedding (and in some cases, that they are also returned on time).

Before the Wedding

It is a good idea for you to make the initial contact with a vendor once they have been chosen, so the vendor will know immediately that you will be the main contact person.

Let's use the wedding cake as an example. Bonnie Bride has decided to go with ABC Bakery for her wedding cake after looking through your vendor portfolio or file. Once Bonnie has met with the bakery representative and picked out the design and type of cake she wants, you take over.

Send a letter on your letterhead to the bakery representative outlining your understanding of the order, the date of the wedding, the venue for drop off and setup of the cake and any other pertinent information. (A sample letter appears on the next page.)

Tell the representative that you are the wedding planner for that particular client and you will be the contact on any matters that arise from this day forward. You might include a copy of the room layout with the cake table clearly marked and any decorating or setup instructions that apply. If the venue is difficult to find, include a map to get there, and make sure the vendor has your cell phone number.

Indicate that your clients are responsible for payment to the vendor including deposits and for any loss or damage to loaned or rented equipment (if applicable).

Send a follow up letter or reminder notice a couple of weeks before the wedding confirming the address and applicable details, such as the time the cake should arrive and setup instructions. Then call the day before the wedding to confirm that everything will go according to plan.

Be prepared with backup plans in the event of unforeseen problems. For example, if the bakery goes out of business a few days before the wedding, you will need to have another bakery you can use.

> **TIP:** In every correspondence with a vendor, state the client's name and wedding date.

Wedding Day Co-ordination

Using the wedding cake as the example, here is what you will do to co-ordinate or liaise with this vendor.

While the bridal party is having their photographs taken (or at another appropriate time) you will connect with the reception venue co-ordinator or caterer and ensure the cake and other items arrived safely and have been set up according to the plan.

Sample Initial Vendor Letter

ABC Bakery
123 Anywhere Road
Small Town, USA

Re: Smith Wedding – June 24, 2006

Dear Billy Baker,

I am writing you today to confirm the arrangements for the Smith wedding, which is to take place June 24, 2006. As Wedding Planner for Jack and Jill, I will be responsible for co-ordination of your services and will now be the contact person on any matters relating to the wedding cake. My understanding of the arrangements is as follows:

- Wedding cake will be delivered to:
  The Central Park Hotel
  1131 Central Park Avenue
  Aspen Room (room layout attached)

- Cake to be delivered and set up by 3:30 p.m.

- Setup and decoration of cake table as discussed with Jill Smith to include fresh blackberries, pink roses and candles

My clients (Jack and Jill Smith) are responsible for payment to you for all services rendered including deposits and for any charges for cancellation of your service. I will be sending a follow up letter to you two weeks before the wedding to ensure everything is in place and on schedule.

Please feel free to contact me when/if the need arises. My contact information is as follows:

Address: Wonderful Weddings
255 Willow Tree Lane
Anytown, USA
Phone: (888) 555-1212
Cell: (888) 555-1234
E-mail: wendy@wonderfulweddings.wen

I look forward to working with your company again and I know the Smiths will be delighted with their cake.

Sincerely,
Wendy Wedding Planner
Wonderful Weddings

You will also do a visual check once you arrive at the reception venue. If the instructions were not followed, fix the situation yourself if you can, or call the contact number and ask the bakery to correct the situation. Make a note of the problem that occurred and another note to remind yourself to follow-up with the vendor.

Again, have a back-up plan in case the cake does not arrive and you cannot reach anyone at the bakery. Is there another bakery nearby that can deliver? Can the venue supply a cake? Can you find an artificial cake to use for photos? Make sure you have your back-up plans in place (for all vendors) well before the wedding day.

If Something Goes Wrong

A few words about respect are necessary here. As essential as it is to be friendly to the management or owners it is also equally important to be friendly and patient with their employees. Vendors have refused to do work for wedding planners for shoddy treatment of their employees.

Mistakes do happen, and while it's all too easy to assign blame, get the facts before you act. For instance, if the limousine company goes to the wrong pick up spot, yelling at the driver is not going to help matters any. You will look unprofessional and in fact, it may not be their fault. You or your assistant may have transposed numbers when typing the address. First and foremost, solve the immediate crisis.

Once the wedding is over, take the matter up in a calm professional manner with the manager or owner at a meeting or phone call set up for this purpose. Work with the management to find a solution for future events and send a follow-up letter outlining your understanding of the events and steps being taken to avoid a future mistake. If a similar incident happens again you would be wise to stop using that vendor. This is a great time to remind you to always carry a cell phone and backup battery for those little emergencies that will happen.

Above all, remember that this is a joyous occasion. If you are upset and ranting you will get everyone around you upset. Your reputation is at stake as well and it would be prudent of you to keep your temper under control. Your job is to provide order and calm to what can be a very stressful day. The advice from a popular antiperspirant advertisement says it best: "Never let them see you sweat."

2.6.4 Follow Up

As soon as possible after the wedding, write thank-you notes where appropriate and follow-up letters of complaint where problems occurred to all of the vendors used for the wedding.

Thank-you notes should be warmly worded and addressed to the owner/ manager. In addition, you should specifically acknowledge any employees who went out of their way to provide excellent service in the letter to the manager and send a thank-you note to the employee as well. (Remember, word of mouth is the best advertising tool you can employ and most of these people will either get married or know someone who will.) An example of a thank-you note appears on the next page.

Complaint letters are a little trickier to word without sounding unreasonable and should never be written in anger. You may want to still maintain a business relationship with the vendor if the problem was with one of their employees, so before closing the door you should give them an opportunity to rectify the situation. The letter should be addressed to the manager/owner and never to the specific employee you may have had the problem with. You should, however, include that individual's name and as many specifics about the situation as you can recall.

If you don't feel comfortable writing a complaint letter, pick up the telephone and speak with the owner or manager about the situation.

Relationship Building

The relationship you build with vendors is critical and will not only be rewarding for both parties but vital to your success. Vendors who do their job well make you look good. Furthermore, vendors can refer business to you. If a vendor has customers who mention they are looking for a wedding planner, you could be the one they recommend. (Section 5.3.2 has more about getting business through vendors.)

Once in a while you may wish to hold a vendor appreciation event to thank those vendors who refer clients to you and who make your job easier. This could be as simple as renting a hospitality suite at a favorite hotel and hosting a small reception after business hours. Let your imagination and pocket book guide you.

Sample Thank-You Note

Dear Billy Baker,

As wedding planner for the recently married Jack and Jill Smith, I just had to write to thank you and your wonderful staff for the excellent and friendly service afforded my clients. On behalf of the Smiths I want to thank you for not only providing a beautiful wedding cake but for the little extra touches that helped make their wedding day special. The extra roses taped to the candlestick holders made for a stunning table arrangement.

I want to especially thank your assistant, Charles, for the extra care he took handling and setting up the cake. Charles is always pleasant and cool under pressure and a delight to work with.

I look forward to working with your company again soon.

Regards,
Wendy Wedding Planner

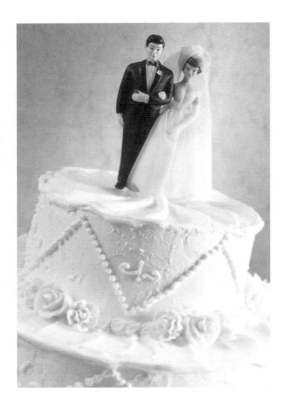

3. Developing Your Skills

Now that you know what the job involves, this chapter will give you information on how to further develop the skills you will need to succeed in this career.

3.1 Do You Have an Aptitude for Wedding Planning?

Wedding planners need to use a variety of skills to do their job well. As you will read in this chapter, all the skills you need to succeed as a wedding planner can be learned. However, if you already have a natural aptitude for planning events, entering this career will be even easier for you.

Here are a couple of ways to determine if you already have the basic skills you will need, or if you will need to brush up on them.

Signs of Wedding Planner Talent

You may already demonstrate some of the talents of a successful wedding planner. If you are suited to a career in wedding planning, your skills have likely shone through in a number of ways. See how many of the following items are true for you:

❑ You like to organize parties and social gatherings.

❑ You are detail-oriented.

❑ You like to plan things in advance and schedule them. You may even keep track of appointments in a day-timer or another scheduler such as a Palm Pilot.

❑ You enjoy handling a number of things all at once.

❑ You are a list maker. (For example, you make grocery lists before you go to the grocery store, you make a list of what to pack before you go on holidays, or you make a list of all the tasks you want to accomplish in a day, etc.)

❑ You can keep calm while multi-tasking.

❑ You are artistic or creative.

❑ You are a natural people person. You enjoy the company of others and like to communicate with people.

❑ You are a romantic at heart.

If you checked off five or more of the above items, chances are you have a talent and natural inclination for the wedding planning profession.

Personality Type

The above list highlights a number of important skills that wedding planners typically have. Many of these skills are typical of people with certain "personality types" as defined by the Myers-Briggs Type Indicator. A renowned system for measuring personality types, it looks at four dimensions of personality:

Extraversion (E)	vs.	Introversion (I)
Sensing (S)	vs.	Intuition (N)
Thinking (T)	vs.	Feeling (F)
Judging (J)	vs.	Perceiving (P)

You can come up with a four letter "personality type" by determining your preferences for each of these four dimensions. Here are a few very basic examples, with the letters in brackets indicating what personality dimension each trait corresponds with.

- "Are you more extraverted (E) or more introverted (I)?"

- "Do you tend to trust your intuition (N) or trust what you see and hear (S)?"

- "Do you focus more on thoughts (T) or feelings (F)?"

- "Do you prefer life to be more structured (J) or more spontaneous (P)?"

There are a variety of ways to learn your own personality type, including being tested by a career counselor, reading a book on personality type, or trying a quick quiz at **www.personalitytype.com/quiz.asp**.

Out of the 16 possible personality types, one that is particularly well suited to wedding planning is ENFJ (**E**xtraverted **IN**tuitive **F**eeling **J**udging). These types of people enjoy to work in an active and challenging environment where they deal with other people they can trust (in the case of wedding planner that may be the vendors you deal with). In addition, they can develop creative solutions to problems, juggle a number of tasks at once and still maintain an orderly environment.

However, it is important to remember that all kinds of people can and do succeed in this career. While someone with an ENFJ or a similar personality type may be more naturally inclined to use such skills, these skills can be learned or developed by any personality type. There are resources in the next section of this guide to assist you with developing these skills.

3.2 Developing Your Skills to Succeed

There are many different skills and traits that can produce a fabulous wedding planner. The skills that are common among the most successful wedding planners are:

- Interpersonal skills

- Organizational skills

- Creativity

Let's take a deeper look at each of these skills, how they relate to being a successful wedding planner, and how you can improve them.

3.2.1 Interpersonal Skills

As a wedding planner, you will not only need to be a good organizer with creative ideas, but you will also need to work effectively with many people (such as the bride and groom, their parents, the bridal attendants, the officiant and numerous vendors) for the wedding to run smoothly.

Accordingly, your interpersonal skills (i.e. your skills in dealing with other people) will be one of the key factors in ensuring that you are successful in the wedding planning profession and ultimately are able to continue to do what you love — wedding planning. Interpersonal skills are important in the wedding planning profession for many reasons. A successful wedding planner must be able to:

- Attract clients

- Successfully communicate with the bride and groom to find out what they want their wedding experience to be so that expectations can be met

- Relate well with others (for example, clients, staff, and the many vendors such as florists, caterers, photographers, etc.) so that the common purpose of producing a successful wedding can be met

Following are some key interpersonal skills and why they can be so helpful to you in the wedding planning profession.

Developing Relationships

To have a flourishing wedding planning business, you first must have clients who will hire you to perform the work. When a bride and groom find out about your services, chances are they will want to meet with you to determine whether there is a "fit" between their needs and your services. If people have a choice between two different wedding planners who both have similar experience and capability, they are more likely to select the wedding planner that they "liked" the most and felt the most comfortable with.

Think about the individuals who you choose to take your business to, such as your hair stylist, your personal trainer (if you have one), the person who runs the corner store, or any of the other individuals that you see regularly to purchase a product or service. For the most part, people prefer to do business with people who they like. Chances are, if you don't like someone or how they treat you, you will take your business somewhere else if you have that option.

If you are able to develop a rapport with people and build their trust in you, they will likely want to hire you to do the job. One of the best ways to get people to like you is to show genuine interest in them.

Dale Carnegie, the author of *How to Win Friends and Influence People*, advises individuals to always ask others about themselves. People love to talk about themselves and have an interested listener. Most couples who are about to be married would love to tell you how they met and fell in love, where they got engaged, etc. Make sure to ask your clients about these things. This is a great way to develop rapport. If you show interest in them, they are more likely going to show interest in you and want to hire you to plan their wedding.

Besides developing relationships with clients, wedding planners will also need to develop relationships with the many vendors that they deal with. The vendors are the individuals you will hire to perform many of the services or provide products that are required to pull off a successful wedding such as a printer, caterer, baker, florist, photographer, videographer, limousine driver, etc. You will need to rely on these individuals to do their part, in a timely manner, so that the wedding runs smoothly.

One thing you may want to do to develop good relationships with vendors is ensure that you either phone them to personally thank them or send them a quick handwritten thank-you note each time after they have provided a service or product for one of the weddings you have planned (even though it is something they are paid for).

Another idea is to find out a little bit about the various vendors' families and to ask about their family when you are in touch with them to order a product or to hire them to provide a service. Most people feel much more kinship with those business associates who ask about their family and how their kids are doing (by name) than others who don't take the time to ever ask. By following these techniques, vendors are much more likely to remember you with kindness.

If you have a good relationship with the vendors, they are more likely to come through or help you get what you want when you need something in a rush or when you need something that is difficult to track down. A vendor who has a good relationship with you is much more likely to go the extra mile for you, which will in turn make you look good to your clients. Just as importantly, vendors can recommend your services to couples who are looking for a wedding planner!

Effective Communication

To be able to co-ordinate a dream wedding for your clients, you will need to find out from them exactly what they want for their wedding and be able to communicate that to others involved with the wedding (such as the officiant and the vendors) so that they understand it. Effective communication involves having good verbal skills, exceptional listening skills and being able to read people.

Verbal Skills

Good verbal skills are helpful when you are selling yourself to potential clients or when you need to communicate the "wedding picture" to the various vendors. Many people prefer to work with somebody they can understand who "speaks their language." To improve your verbal communication skills, ask friends or a vocal coach for feedback on any areas that could be improved, such as: clarity of speech, use of slang, proper grammar, or altering your tone of voice to eliminate any harshness. (You can find vocal coaches in the Yellow Pages.)

Listening

Being an excellent listener is key to providing your clients with the wedding they want. When you meet with them, ask them to envision their ideal wedding and communicate that to you. As they speak, make sure that you are really listening to what they have to say.

While listening seems like an easy skill to master, most of us experience challenges in at least one of the following areas involved in listening:

- Paying attention

- Understanding

- Remembering

You can improve your listening skills by focusing fully on someone when they are speaking, asking clarifying questions if you don't understand, paraphrasing (repeating back to them what you thought you heard), and taking notes. There are numerous books on the subject of honing your listening skills and one of the best is *Listening: The Forgotten Skill (A Self-Teaching Guide)*, by Madelyn Burley-Allen. Helpful free advice is available online at **www.businesslistening.com**.

Reading People

In addition to hearing what people say, a skilled wedding planner also notices non-verbal communication. Being able to "read" people can not only help you get the job, it can help ensure you keep your clients satisfied. For example, did a prospective client fold their arms when you made a particular suggestion? If so, they may be communicating that they disagree, even if they don't actually say so.

Although body language can't tell you precisely what someone is thinking, it can give you clues so you can ask follow-up questions, even as basic as "How do you feel about that?"

If you want to improve this skill, you can find some excellent advice in books such as *Reading People,* by Jo-Ellan Dimitrius and *How to Read a Person Like a Book*, by Gerald I. Nierenberg and Henry H. Calero.

Negotiation

As soon as clients or potential employers decide they would like to work with you, you will be faced with the issue of how much you will get paid. You will find information about standard fees for wedding planners later in this guide. However, no matter what fees are "standard," you may be able to get paid more through effective negotiation skills.

Also, being a good negotiator can help you save money on vendors' products or services such as flowers, photographs, venue rentals, etc. The money that you save can either be passed on to your clients or could be part of the additional income that you receive as a wedding planner, depending on your arrangement.

While vendors that you work with frequently might offer discounts to you, there may be occasions when you need to work with a vendor chosen by your clients, and the vendor may not be used to giving discounts to wedding planners they have not worked with in the past. In these cases, being a good negotiator may help you and your clients save money.

You can find some excellent tips for negotiating in section 2.6 (Working with Vendors). If you want some additional advice to help you improve your negotiating skills, one book that is especially helpful is *Get Anyone to Do Anything*, by David J. Lieberman.

3.2.2 Organizational Skills

Being well organized is key to being a successful wedding planner. After all, you are being hired to "organize" a wedding.

As a wedding planner, there will be many times that you will have to juggle quite a few tasks and deal with numerous people (the bride and groom, their attendants, the officiant and the vendors) all at the same time. It will be crucial to ensure that the many tasks and details are handled in a timely manner so that the wedding runs smoothly.

If you want to improve your organizational skills, you will find practical advice from professional organizer and author Maria Gracia on the next three pages.

Expert Advice to Help You Stay Organized

We asked Maria Gracia, owner of Get Organized Now! and author of *Finally Organized, Finally Free*, to share her advice on how you can stay organized as a wedding planner.

What are some good tips to effectively schedule many items and ensure that they are handled in the time frame required?

First, it is imperative to make a written list of everything that needs to be done. Just put the tasks in any order initially, then spend some time prioritizing them. Sometimes it's easier to first write each task on an index card, along with the approximate timeframe prior to the wedding (six months prior, two months prior, three weeks prior, etc.) that each task must be completed.

Then, just rearrange the cards. Finally, using your computer word processor, and the index cards, create and print a checklist of these tasks, and save it as your Master Planning Checklist.

Print one of those checklists out for each bride, and insert each into its own binder labeled with the bride's name and wedding date. You now have a list you can check off for each bride as tasks are completed.

Using one calendar and your checklist, begin scheduling in the tasks you must complete each day. It is recommended that you use a Daily Calendar for this purpose, as you'll be writing in a number of tasks — especially if you're assisting more than three or four brides at a time.

What is the best way to stay organized and on top of the "wedding plan" and what are some tips for multi-tasking and ensuring that nothing is missed when you have many items to handle all at once?

Again, the magic trick is to use a physical checklist that is prioritized in the order the tasks must be done. Be sure that you're checking off tasks as they are completed.

One of my best tips is to remain calm. It's very easy to get frazzled, especially when the bride is nervous, and the big day has arrived. In the end, if you've done your homework, things will fall into place nicely. Expect snags. They will happen. As long as you expect obstacles and have some back-up plans in place, you'll ensure that everything will be as smooth as possible.

As a wedding planner, there are many different individuals you need to "organize" and work with, such as the bridal party, the officiant, the musicians, the caterer, the decorator, etc. What is the best way to keep everyone "organized" to have a successful wedding?

A good plan of attack is vital. Therefore, it's very important to work out all of the details way ahead of time and to meet with each person involved, taking very good notes along the way.

I would strongly recommend that the bride and each of her attendants (in addition to the groom and his attendants) gets a list of their responsibilities, detailing the responsibility and where in the schedule that responsibility falls, so everyone knows what's next. A wedding should be basically like a well-orchestrated play, and everyone should know their "part."

It's also a good idea to delegate whenever possible, since you can't be in two places at one time. For instance, a wedding planner can assign certain tasks to each bridesmaid. One can be on the lookout for the arrival of the flowers. One can direct the photographer to the appropriate people so photos can be started quickly. Of course, each of those bridesmaids should be instructed to report back to you, so you are aware of everything going on.

For the bridal planner, it is imperative that they know everything that is going on, and who is responsible for what. So, be sure to have a schedule of events for each wedding, clearly listing the events, and people involved next to each. It is also strongly recommended that one or two rehearsals are held ahead of time. This will further ensure that everyone understands the sequence and details of each event.

Do you have any other organizational tips that may be helpful to the readers of this guide?

1. Plan well ahead of time.

The further in advance you plan, the better off you'll be. Of course, you'll have to confirm details as the big day nears, but planning well ahead will give you a sense of calmness and order along the way, and will ensure you're able to make reservations with those reception halls, vendors, etc. that are your first choice.

2. Use project binders.

Use a 1/2" binder for every bride you're working with, and keep thorough notes. Organize the contents of that binder with index dividers separated by major categories: Church, Reception, Invitations, Vendors, etc. Include pocket folders in each section for smaller items, like receipts or brochures. Now you'll have an excellent resource for each bride, and a place to keep your notes.

3. Keep an idea book.

As you attend weddings yourself, or watch wedding movies and/or videos, you'll begin to collect a number of ideas for themes, favors, toasts, etc. Use an idea book, binder, or your computer if you prefer, to keep a log of these ideas. You'll end up with an excellent reference resource.

4. Have an effective filing system.

Since you're going to be dealing with so many people on a regular basis — caterers, florists, limousine companies, etc. — an effective filing system can go a long way. You'll need at least one large four-drawer filing cabinet to store all of your reference materials and catalogs. Keep the contents of your filing cabinet up-to-date by weeding it out at least once every six months. This will give you room for new companies and new ideas. Also, office supply stores sell binders that have tabs on the spine, which allows them to sit perfectly in a filing cabinet if you wish to store your brides' binders that way.

Samples of a time-line schedule and checklists are included in chapter 2 of this guide. You can find additional helpful advice in Maria Gracia's book Finally Organized, Finally Free.

3.2.3 Creativity

Getting married is a major milestone in most people's lives and their wedding is something they will want to remember for a lifetime. As a wedding planner, you will need to use your creativity to come up with unique ideas for ceremonies and receptions even if you are hired to put on a "traditional" wedding. After all, each couple that hires you will be different from the next and they will want to have some elements of their wedding that are special to them.

If you are hired to put on a non-traditional wedding, chances are you will have even more opportunities to put your creative ideas to use (particularly if you have been hired to plan a theme wedding). The amount of creativity and "uniqueness" you will add to each wedding will depend on the desires of the bride and groom.

Many people believe that creativity is something you are either born with or not. However, experts say that creativity can be taught and, more importantly, can be learned. Following are some suggestions for how you can get your creative juices flowing.

Brainstorm

Sit down with others involved with your wedding business, and try to come up with as many new wedding ideas as you can. To brainstorm effectively, make sure that there is a continuous flowing of ideas without any judgment and that the ideas are not discussed until all ideas have been stated. (Ideally, one person should be keeping track of them and writing them down.)

When you let yourself talk and blurt out ideas without thinking about them, the most amazing and creative ideas can start to come out. After you have your list of ideas, you can then discuss them and you will be surprised at how many good ideas come out as you discuss the list.

Leave a Note Pad by Your Bed

Write down any ideas that come to you as you are drifting off to sleep or when you first awake in the morning. It is proven that the brain is considered to be more creative when it is in the "Alpha" state (just before falling asleep and immediately after waking up and also while dreaming).

Think Outside of the Box

Consider alternative ways of doing things. For example, if the wedding couple wants a unique processional and asks you to come up with some ideas, you can throw out the traditional rules.

One of the authors of this guide was involved with an outdoor wedding in a park where the groom, dressed in 19th century formalwear, was escorted down the aisle with a violinist playing a beautiful piece of music after his 13 groomsmen (including one woman) had walked down the aisle.

The bride only wanted one attendant and arrived by horsedrawn carriage with her attendant and father and was dropped off at the beginning of the aisle. It was a unique and memorable wedding and it was perfect for the bride and groom.

Other Ideas

- **Flip through magazines.** In addition to bridal magazines, look through publications such as *People*, *Town & Country*, *Good Housekeeping* and decorating magazines to get ideas from what you see. Use an idea book to keep track of any great ideas for themes, table centerpieces, favors, etc.

- **Watch movies for theme ideas.** For example, if you are planning a beach party theme wedding, rent beach party movies. Or if you have a western theme wedding to plan, watch a couple of old western movies. One of the authors of this guide planned a wedding for a couple who decided to get married in Virginia City (an old west town in Nevada) and they sent out invitations with burnt edges that were rolled into a scroll. They looked fabulous and gave the guests an idea of what was to come.

- **Check out websites**. You will find a variety of sites mentioned throughout this guide. You may get ideas either from major wedding websites (see the next section) or from other wedding planners' websites. (Sometimes the best ideas come from witnessing what others do.) While you wouldn't want to copy what they do, you might pick up some great ideas that you could modify.

Besides using your artistic creativity to come up with unique ideas for theme weddings or to decorate a reception venue beautifully or to create wonderful table centerpieces or favors, etc., you will also need to use your creativity when problems or delays arise.

As mentioned in the section on working with vendors, no matter how much planning you do in advance, there is still the possibility that others may not come through and, in some cases, you may need to use your creative problem-solving skills to quickly come up with alternative arrangements.

3.3 Teaching Yourself Wedding Planning

As most self-made businesspeople will tell you, there are ways other than traditional schooling to learn how to become accomplished in the career of your dreams, and this especially holds true for becoming a wedding planner. While it's true you could choose to learn through either traditional methods (e.g. taking a course at a local college) or non-traditional methods (e.g. distance learning), you can also acquire the necessary skills by teaching yourself.

In this section you will find a variety of ways to teach yourself wedding planning by observing, listening, reading, and doing.

> **TIP:** Although this section is devoted to self-teaching, even those who choose to go the conventional educational route will find the ensuing advice helpful.

3.3.1 Places to Go

Weddings

The most logical place to begin learning about planning weddings is to observe weddings. Although it may sound obvious, it is nonetheless critical to attend as many weddings as possible. This is probably not a tough assignment for you, as most wedding planners have one thing in common: they LOVE weddings.

So, how do you find weddings to observe? If you come from a large family, this should be relatively easy as you will most likely be invited to attend quite a number of weddings. If you come from a small family and don't have a large circle of friends getting married in the near future, ask everyone you know if it would be okay for you to tag along or be their guest at an upcoming wedding they have been invited to. Now is not the time to be shy!

If you are even slightly acquainted with the bride or groom ask if they would allow you to sit in during the ceremony only. This will not cost them anything and in fact, they may feel flattered that you care enough to want to attend.

In particular, try to attend weddings of people with different ethnic and religious backgrounds than you. Once you've started planning weddings, if you can advertise that you are aware of the wedding customs followed by Japanese, Pakistani, Irish, Russian, Greek and Caribbean peoples and/or of the Jewish, Catholic, Buddhist and Muslim faiths, you will definitely have a leg up on your competition.

Make sure you treat attending the wedding as a business assignment and remember you are there to gather facts. Take a small notebook and unobtrusively jot down a few notes about how the ceremony was handled, what traditions were observed, how long the ceremony was and anything else you can think of that would be useful when planning a wedding. Pay particular attention to anything new, unusual or trendy.

Bridal Shows or Fairs

One of the first events the newly engaged bride-to-be and her friends or bridal party attend is a local *bridal fair*, or *bridal show* as they are sometimes called. Bridal fairs are in essence a trade show for every conceivable business even remotely connected to the bridal industry.

Typically, these shows will take place in the early part of the year (January, February or March) to take advantage of not only the next year's wedding season but for any last-minute shopping for the upcoming wedding months (May, June, July and August). They are held year round in some locations. You can find them by doing an online search for "bridal fair" or "bridal show" and the name of your city.

Products and services showcased at a bridal fair include: wedding and attendant fashions (often highlighted by a fashion show), wedding planners, lingerie designers and retailers, esthetician services, travel agents, florists, cake bakers and decorators, limousine rental companies, caterers and venue operators.

When you attend a bridal show, observe what booths, services or fashions generate the most excitement. Is one venue more popular than the others? What honeymoon locale are travel agents booking most frequently this year? What baker, florist, or designer is hot or in the news? Ask questions at every booth and keep as many notes as possible. Remember, you are teaching yourself and at the end of the day you will not receive notes to take home unless you create them.

When you come across a competitor's booth (another wedding planner), at the very least, take a business card and brochure. If a website is not posted on the card, ask if they have one and note it on the business card. Jot down any great marketing ideas you observe and information on fees and services provided. Keep them together with the business cards in a file on your competitors.

3.3.2 People to Speak With

As you prepare for your new career, look for opportunities to speak with and learn from brides-to-be and other groups involved in the planning and execution of a wedding. Here are some specific ways to speak with these groups, at bridal fairs and elsewhere.

Competitors

When attending a bridal fair, you should use the event as an opportunity to speak with as many wedding planners as possible. If you have not set up your business yet and are still in the fact-gathering stage, you might act as though you are interested in possibly hiring a planner or co-ordinator and ask a few interview questions as you would if you were really planning on hiring one.

One very important point to remember, though, is that these people have paid for a table or booth at the fair and are there to find new paying clients. You may be wasting their time if you have no intention of hiring them, and in fact you may lose a possible mentor or apprentice opportunity if you are not respectful of their time.

Vendors

One of the best ways to learn about all aspects of the wedding business is by speaking with vendors. After all, they are experts in their respective areas.

For example, a florist could give you detailed information about all the flowers needed for a typical wedding (bouquets, corsages, boutonnieres, flower arrangements for the ceremony and reception, etc.), approximate costs, how far ahead to order, what is most popular with brides, and anything else you would need to know about wedding flowers.

As mentioned above, you can find many vendors with booths at bridal fairs. However, vendors that have paid to participate in a bridal show are there because they want to sell their products or services. While they may be able to speak with you briefly, you will likely have a better opportunity to learn from them if you take their business cards and make appointments to meet later.

You don't have to wait for a bridal fair to find vendors to speak with. You can find vendors online, in the Yellow Pages, or through word of mouth. Listen twice as much as you speak at vendor interviews, as these people have most likely done numerous weddings and can pass on many valuable tips to you. For advice on how to contact vendors and gather information from them, refer to the advice in section 2.6.1.

Brides

One of the most efficient ways to meet as many brides-to-be as possible at one time is to visit bridal fairs. Speaking with them can give you some insights into what brides are looking for, what they are experiencing as they plan their weddings, and why they are (or are not) using the services of a wedding planner.

You can also learn a lot from recent brides. When you hear of someone who is recently married, ask if they will free up a bit of time for a short chat or interview with you. Ask them what went wrong, what went right and why, what they would change given the chance and what they wish their wedding planner would have done for them.

If they didn't use the services of a planner, find out why. This is as important as knowing why they did use one. Once you have started a wedding planning business (see chapter 5) you will inevitably be asked, during your initial consultation with prospective clients, why someone should use your services. You'll want to be prepared.

For instance, finding out that the limo company failed to show up at the bride's home for the drive to the church because no one actually asked them to be there (true story) can be used as an example of why a wedding planner is valuable. What bride wants to be left standing at her door or having to call a taxi at the last minute?

If you do not know of any recent brides, many bridal websites offer a section with tips and advice from brides who have already tied the knot. USABrides.com has a wonderful forum and article section called *Talk About Weddings* at **www.talkaboutweddings.com**. This is a great way to get into the minds and hearts of brides and find out what they're talking about, what they want and emerging trends.

Ministers, Rabbis and Priests

Ministers, rabbis and priests are the absolute experts at what should, and should never, happen during a wedding ceremony.

If you can arrange short interviews with various members of the clergy you will learn more about ceremonies than you could from many books and classes put together. These individuals have seen it all, from the dull to the spectacular.

Start by asking your clergy person for an interview. If you do not attend religious services, ask for a referral from your parents, family, friend or a neighbor. When requesting an interview, remember that these people are extremely busy and inundated with demands on their time, so keep your questions to the point, on topic and don't overstay your welcome.

In chapter 2 you saw some questions to ask when you are looking to hire an officiant for a wedding ceremony. At this stage your questions will be focused on helping you learn, so questions you might ask could include:

- What are the traditions of that particular faith that should be observed during the ceremony?

- What are the most common mistakes made by the bride and groom?

- What advice would he/she like to give regarding the ceremony?

- Is there a standard fee for officiating at the ceremony? How should it be paid?

- How can a wedding planner be most useful to them at the ceremony?

- Are they willing to perform a service outside of their home church (either in another facility or outdoors)?

- Will they perform a ceremony with another clergy present? (Sometimes couples in mixed-faith marriages request that clergy from both faiths bless the marriage.)

A Mixed-Faith Wedding

Kennedy and Jaesen, a mixed-faith couple, were torn between being married in the Catholic or United church. Neither person had strong ties to either community but also didn't feel ready to commit or convert to just one or the other.

The solution: a wonderful minister in the Baptist faith. When asked if he would perform the service on neutral ground (the beautiful dining room of an inn overlooking a lake) he replied that he would be honored to.

It could be argued that you shouldn't need to know these details until you are working for a client from that faith. However, it puts you ahead of your competitors if you are already familiar with different services and indeed have made contacts with clergy from each faith.

Having this knowledge ahead of time – that the Baptist minister would perform the service outside of his church and for a mixed-faith couple – saved countless hours of anxiety and tension for the bride and groom. A wedding planner can help ward off potential problems by offering options that the couple may not have considered.

3.3.3 Things to Do

We've all heard of the conundrum: No one will hire me without experience but I can't get experience without first getting a job. Fortunately, you can get wedding experience before someone hires you to plan their wedding. Here are some possibilities.

Plan Weddings for Family and Friends

Once you've attended a few weddings and followed the excellent advice and information you learned in this guide you should be ready to plan a wedding. So, who is going to trust their most precious day to a beginner? Someone who knows you, of course!

Almost all of us have family and friends who are either planning a wedding sometime in the future or are in the middle of planning a wedding right now. This presents you with a great opportunity to get your first "client." Ask those close to you if you could be their wedding planner. Even if you can't secure a paid arrangement, at least assist for free in the planning of their wedding. After all, you do not have to get paid to plan a wedding to be considered the "wedding planner."

So, how do you convince family and friends that you are right for the job? This is where your powers of persuasion and the proof of all your research come in. Before you approach anyone you should have your planning system set up. When you meet with them, explain the benefits of having you plan their wedding, including how you can help them save time and money. Be prepared for any questions that might arise and be ready to share a couple of ideas with the couple.

Even if you are volunteering your services, you will want to be as organized and businesslike as possible to ensure you will be taken seriously. Dress professionally and present yourself and your ideas as confidently as you can. Follow the advice in section 5.4 on working with clients.

Your role, in these first couple of weddings, can be as simple as shopping for accessories with the bride or helping co-ordinate the wedding party on the actual wedding day, or as complicated as full service wedding planning from start to finish.

There is no right or wrong way to gain experience and the smallest service you provide may assist you in getting future wedding planning work. If you feel confident enough to shop, compare, suggest and contact the various vendors, go ahead and offer to take this on. Just remember not to offer to do more than you feel absolutely comfortable doing. It would be far better to do a bang-up job with a smaller list of items then to forget things on a much larger list.

When you have been hired as the wedding planner, be as professional as you possibly can. Do not get into petty arguments with the bride (even if she's your brother's intended and you don't see eye to eye). Remember, first and foremost, that this is not your wedding. Even if the bride has decided to have orange-and-black bridesmaids' dresses and you feel the whole affair will look like a scene from a bad Halloween movie, keep quiet. You can gently try to steer her towards a more pleasing color combination, but in the end you must accept her wishes.

Let the couple know in advance that you will want some photographs of the wedding for your "portfolio" (a collection of samples to show to future clients). After the wedding you can also ask for a letter of recommendation. Section 5.3.1 explains how to prepare a portfolio and get letters of recommendation.

Learn from a Pro

If you have the opportunity, spending time with an experienced wedding planner can be a tremendously valuable learning experience. Imagine being present during client consultations and vendor meetings and, even more importantly, having the opportunity to attend real weddings to see how it all comes together.

The added bonus of working with an experienced planner is that they might be open to bringing in a partner or hiring additional staff in the future. If you get along well with the person and are able to show what a valuable asset you'd be, you could be a shoe-in for a permanent job.

One way to learn from a pro is to volunteer your services. A busy wedding planner might be able to use help with tasks such as running errands, making decorations, staffing a booth at a bridal fair, etc. Depending on your schedule and the wedding planner's needs, you could offer your services free of charge for a few months.

Another way to learn is through "job shadowing." This involves spending a day, a week, or some other limited period of time observing someone work. It allows you to learn more about a career, ask questions, and actually see what a job entails on a daily basis. Most positions are arranged through personal connections or networking, so ask for recommendations from friends and family who have used the services of a wedding planner. Make sure you mention the name of the mutual friend or client when calling to ask for an appointment.

If you can't get a personal referral, you could try contacting wedding planners you find online or in your local phone book (search under "Weddings" in the Yellow Pages). Be prepared that some wedding planners may not be keen to help train a potential competitor; however, a successful wedding planner may be so busy they will be happy to have your help.

If you can't find a wedding planner in your area that will either agree to act as a mentor or let you job shadow, try calling event planners. Tell them you are interested in planning weddings but would be open to planning any event they need assistance with. Planning any event will be a tremendous help to you. Start by checking the local Yellow Pages, or doing an online search for "event planners" plus the name of your city. Hundreds of event planners can also be found by searching the International Special Events Society website at **www.ises.com**.

Another possibility is to try calling bridal chapels and other wedding venues and ask the on-site wedding co-ordinator if it would be possible to job-shadow or help them with a couple of events (free of charge, of course). This will give you the opportunity to learn more about the business and also to observe weddings.

If you are smart you will also use this opportunity as a networking or resource-building occasion. The more people in the industry you develop a relationship with, the better.

Get a Part-Time Job

Another good way to get related experience is by taking a part-time job with a company involved in the wedding industry. Even if the job doesn't focus on wedding planning, it may give you an opportunity to learn more about weddings. For example, you could apply to work with a bridal shop, caterer, florist, formalwear store, reception venue, etc. Chapter 4 covers the many career opportunities in the wedding industry.

3.3.4　What to Read and Watch

The public is fascinated by weddings. So it's not surprising that the media (television, newspapers, magazines, movies, books and the Internet) provide us with plenty of coverage of weddings — both real and fantasy. While media such as books and websites can be excellent resources for learning wedding planning, even television and movies can give you some great ideas for weddings.

Magazines

If you visit your local newsstand you will find numerous bridal magazines. The most popular U.S. magazines include *Bride's*, *Bridal Guide*, and *Modern Bride*, while the top Canadian magazines are *Today's Bride* and *Wedding Bells*. You can also find local magazines in many cities.

Most bridal magazines are jam-packed with helpful how-to articles, ideas, and advertisements. Pick up a selection of magazines from your local magazine store, visit their websites, or browse them for free at your local public library.

Television

Television's TLC (The Learning Channel) programming includes a videography of weddings called *A Wedding Story* (check your local listings for times). While these stories are definitely edited and don't usually show weddings that went completely off the rails they are interesting to watch and are a great source of ideas.

What you will see is that not all weddings are picture perfect and that even if the bride shows up 20 minutes late, or the maid-of-honor is too sick to attend, or the baker drops the cake while setting it up, most weddings can be salvaged.

Movies

There is also no shortage of movies about weddings. Among the film classics that feature a wedding are *Fiddler on the Roof, The Godfather, Gone with the Wind, Hello Dolly!, High Society, Love Story, The Sound of Music*, and *Steel Magnolias*. More recent wedding flicks include *My Big Fat Greek Wedding, My Best Friend's Wedding, The Best Man, Muriel's Wedding, Runaway Bride,* and *The Wedding Singer*. For inspiration, here are a few of our favorite wedding movies:

- **Father of the Bride**
  Starring Steve Martin, Diane Keaton, Kimberly Williams, and the hilarious Martin Short as a wedding planner named Franc. A remake of the 1950 classic starring Elizabeth Taylor and Spencer Tracy.

- **Four Weddings and a Funeral**
  Nominated for a best picture Oscar, this British production stars Hugh Grant and Andie MacDowell.

- **The Wedding Planner**
  This is our top pick for anyone who wants to become a wedding planner. Starring Jennifer Lopez as a wedding planner who is a creative, incredibly organized, solution-oriented, compassionate communicator that can work miracles so that everything runs smoothly at a wedding. Complications arise when she falls for a groom played by Matthew McConaughey.

The Internet

The Internet is a wonderful learning tool providing instant access to people and services all over the world. However, the amount of information available online can sometimes be overwhelming. For example, if you type "weddings" into the Google search engine, you will find there are more than two million websites on the topic!

To save you time, below is a short list of recommended websites. Many have checklists, and some offer free interactive wedding planners you can use to keep track of the budget, timelines, guest list, gifts, etc.

- *Bliss Weddings*
  www.blissweddings.com

- *Frugal Bride*
  www.frugalbride.com

- *ForeverWed.com*
  www.foreverwed.com

- *The Knot*
  www.theknot.com

- *Top 100 Wedding Sites*
  www.top100weddingsites.com

- *UltimateWedding.com*
  www.ultimatewedding.com

- *USABride.com*
  www.usabride.com

- *Wedding Basics*
  www.weddingbasics.com

- *WeddingChannel.com*
  www.weddingchannel.com

The USABride site also has a number of free newsletters available on a wide variety of subjects. They are delivered daily via e-mail. You can sign up at **www.usabride.com/newsletter**.

> **TIP:** Some future brides may feel, given the abundance of re-sources available free on the Internet, that they can cut out the services of a planner. If you are meeting with prospective clients who bring up this point, you can remind them that co-ordinating your own wedding — no matter what tools you use — still leaves a burden of responsibility on the bride and groom's shoulders.

Books

While bookstores carry a vast number of books on weddings, it can be quite costly to build a substantial library. For a low-cost alternative, don't forget to check out your local library for any of these or similar books. Here are just a few of the many wonderful books on the subject of weddings:

- *The Best of Martha Stewart Living: Weddings*, by Martha Stewart

- *Emily Post's Wedding Etiquette: Cherished Traditions and Contemporary Ideas for a Joyous Celebration,* by Peggy Post

- *Great Wedding Tips from the Experts*, by Robbi Ernst III

- *Miss Manners on Weddings*, by Judith Martin

- *The Knot Guide to Wedding Vows and Traditions: Readings, Rituals, Music, Dances, Speeches and Toasts*, by Carley Roney

- *The Knot Ultimate Wedding Planner: Worksheets, Checklists, Etiquette, Calendars, & Answers to Frequently Asked Questions*, by Carley Roney

3.4 Educational Programs

It is certainly possible to have a career in wedding planning without taking any educational or professional development programs. However, you will likely be able to learn about wedding planning more quickly and thoroughly from experts by taking some form of wedding planning education. Otherwise, you may find that you learn some things the hard way — by making mistakes that could have been avoided.

If your plan is to do wedding planning more as a non-paid hobby than as a profession, and you have experience with planning weddings for family members or friends, then any further education may not be desired or required. However, if you do plan to grow a professional wedding planning business, further education would definitely be an asset to give you more knowledge and credibility and to show your clients that you are serious about your profession.

In addition to offering on-site programs (where students attend classes in person), a number of organizations also offer wedding planning programs through distance learning. Distance learning may take the form of correspondence courses, where you receive materials by mail and can work at home, at any time of the day, and at your own pace.

Another type of distance education is online learning. With online learning you will typically enroll at the same time as other students and must meet course deadlines. Online learning allows you to interact with instructors and other classmates through chat sessions and e-mail.

3.4.1 What to Look For

To start with, what you should look for in a program will depend on you and your preferences.

- Do you enjoy attending classes so you can interact with other people? Or do you prefer to work at your own pace? If you prefer to set your own pace, a distance learning program will suit you better than a program offered in a traditional classroom setting.

- How much time and money do you want to invest in your education? You could spend anywhere from a few hours to several years, and anywhere from a couple of hundred dollars to a couple of thousand dollars, on your education.

These are factors to consider when you are evaluating different programs. In addition to your personal preferences, there are several questions you can ask to make you feel comfortable with the quality of a particular program.

In this section we list a variety of educational programs. However, we cannot say which program, if any, will be best for you. You are the only one who can make that decision. You can ask some of the following questions and see if it is possible for you to speak with the instructor and former graduates of the program.

Is the Program Accredited?

Many education programs are accredited by official organizations such as Accrediting Commission of the Distance Education and Training

Council. Accreditation means that the program has met certain educational standards. (However, even if a program is not accredited, you may still find it to be valuable, depending on your personal goals.)

Is the Program Recognized in the Profession?

This question is best asked of people who are working in the profession. If you are talking with professional wedding planners (at a bridal fair, for example), you can ask them if they have heard of a program you are considering and, if so, what their opinion is.

What Does the Program Cover?

You may be able to save yourself some disappointment by finding out in advance what topics you will be expected to learn. If you want to focus on starting and marketing a wedding planning business you may not be happy with a program that simply covers how to plan a wedding.

Who is Offering the Program?

Find out who is teaching the course. What are their credentials? How long have they been a wedding planner or consultant? Do they have previous teaching experience? If you are taking a program from a company, find out how long they have been in business. You can also contact the Better Business Bureau. They can tell you whether there are any complaints lodged against the company.

3.4.2 Certificate Programs

A variety of organizations offer certificate programs in *Wedding Consulting* (sometimes called *Bridal Consulting* or *Wedding Planning*). The number of courses you must complete to earn a certificate will vary from one educational institution to another.

In this section you will find a list of wedding consulting programs you can take from home. These programs teach standard wedding planning such as co-ordinating the ceremony and reception, wedding etiquette, etc. Most also teach various business aspects of wedding consulting, such as setting up your own wedding planning business, marketing, consulting with clients, etc.

When considering costs, keep in mind that some programs will let you pay in installments so that you can spread out payments over a period of months (you should verify this in advance). Also, some correspondence programs charge a nominal fee (e.g. $24 or more) for shipping of materials.

TIP: As mentioned above, we cannot say whether any of the programs listed in this guide will be right for you. You are the only one who can make that decision. Program costs and other details can change, so make sure you confirm information about any program before registering.

The Association of Bridal Consultants

The Association of Bridal Consultants ("ABC") is the leading professional organization for wedding planners, with approximately 4,000 members in 26 countries on six continents including wedding consultants, vendors and corporations. They have one of the most comprehensive professional development programs in the industry.

Website: **www.bridalassn.com**

Program: ABC offers programs leading to three designations (see details below):

• Professional Bridal Consultant

• Accredited Bridal Consultant

• Master Bridal Consultant

Format: Correspondence program
ABC recommends that any individuals interested in starting their own wedding consulting business obtain and work through ABC's start-up manual titled *Weddings as a Business* (which sells for $99) prior to taking the professional development programs.

Contact: E-mail **office@bridalassn.com** or phone (860) 355-0464

Professional Bridal Consultant Program

The *Professional Bridal Consultant™* program is a five-course home study program that can be completed in any sequence and without any time limit (if a member remains in good standing).

There is a final exam at the end of the program. The topics covered are etiquette (including planning the "perfect" wedding), sales and marketing, wedding day (ceremony and reception information), related services (vendor information) and planning and consulting (including organization and understanding the bride's emotions). The average individual takes about three to six months to complete this program. The cost is $85 for each of the five courses or $340 for the entire program.

Accredited Bridal Consultant Program

After three years as a Professional Bridal Consultant™, an individual can renew that designation (upon successfully completing a proficiency exam) or advance to *Accredited Bridal Consultant™* as long as all of the requirements are met (including completing a proficiency exam and responding to an essay question; participating in an ABC seminar, workshop or annual conference; receiving recommendations from three peers and three clients; and paying the processing fee). The cost to obtain the Accredited Bridal Consultant designation is $75.

Master Bridal Consultant Program

After three years as an Accredited Bridal Consultant™, an individual can renew that designation or advance to *Master Bridal Consultant™* as long as all of the requirements are met. Details can be found at the ABC website under professional education. The cost to obtain the Master Bridal Consultant designation is $100 (after meeting the requirements).

Association of Certified Professional Wedding Consultants

The Association of Certified Professional Wedding Consultants (ACPWC) has been registered with the Department of Consumer Affairs for over 12 years and its school/materials are subject to review annually by the Bureau for Private Postsecondary and Vocational Education.

Website: www.acpwc.com/the_school.html

Program: Level 1: Certificate of Completion

Format: You can take it through correspondence or on-site training programs offered in different U.S. cities throughout the year

Length: Correspondence program allows you to work at your own pace. On-site program is five days (or a four-day extended weekend).

Cost: $795 U.S. for home correspondence program, $895 U.S. for five-day (or four-day extended weekend) program

Contact: E-mail annnola1@earthlink.net or phone (408) 528-9000

The Level 1 Certificate of Completion program covers the things a wedding consultant needs to know to start their business and it also covers all aspects of planning a wedding. A comprehensive workbook, assignments and graduation are included for the on-site program and the workbook, assignments and a video of all class sessions are included with the correspondence program.

The Certificate of Completion is a first step in working towards the ACPWC'S "Professional" or "Certified Wedding Consultant" designations. These are awarded either through Levels II or III of ACPWC's advanced qualification programs as set out at the ACPWC website.

Education Direct

Education Direct, also known as Thomson Education Direct and formerly known as the International Correspondence School (ICS), has been providing numerous diploma programs through distance learning to students around the world for more than 100 years.

Website: www.educationdirect.com/bridalconsultant/

Program: Professional Bridal Consultant Diploma

Format: Correspondence program

Length: You can take as little as six months or up to two years to complete the program.

Cost: The U.S. program costs $798 U.S. for American residents. International rates vary. You can pay in installments.

Contact: E-mail info@educationdirect.com or phone 800-275-4410

The Professional Bridal Consultant Diploma program covers basics of the business, how to set your fees, roles of the consultant, how to organize a wedding, researching caterers, ethnic and specialty weddings, and bridal shows. Plus you'll get tips on running your own successful bridal consultant business and more. The program is endorsed by the Association of Bridal Consultants. With the program you will get books, lessons, learning aids, and special supplements included at no additional cost.

Also, once you have completed the first segment of the program, you can receive a three-month novice membership in the Association of Bridal Consultants, and eligibility for ABC Professional Bridal Consultant status upon graduation. Education Direct also offers toll-free instructional support and access to student services by phone, mail and on their website (including online examinations and account review).

June Wedding, Inc.
An Association for Event Professionals

June Wedding, Inc. offers two Wedding Consultant Certification Programs — one for beginners and an advanced program for individuals who are already wedding consultants. (They also offer a Vendor Certification Program.)

Website: **www.junewedding.com/vendorresources_ certification.html**

Programs: Wedding Consultant Certification Program Seminar I: Designing and Running a Successful Wedding Consultant/Event Co-ordination Company

Wedding Consultant Certification Program Seminar II: Continuing Education For The Advanced Wedding Consultant

Format: Correspondence program plus completion of three telephone consultations (or course is taught on location)

Length: Course to be completed within three months (extensions of six weeks may be granted at an additional fee of $275)

Cost: $1,000 U.S. for either Seminar I or Seminar II (plus postage and telephone fees)

Contact: E-mail robbi@junewedding.com or phone (469) 241-1480. (It is suggested you refer to the website for more information.)

Seminar I: Designing & Running a Successful Wedding Consultant/Event Co-ordination Company

This seminar is geared towards new wedding consultants and addresses the fundamentals of owning your own business including starting, designing and running a successful wedding/event consultant company, budgeting, marketing, pricing, establishing reception sites, setting up files and portfolios on vendors and practical hands-on applications to teach you how to successfully negotiate and co-ordinate contracts, schedules, budgets, payment and floor plans (a student manual is provided).

Successful completion of Seminar I leads to certification and designation as a Professional Wedding Consultant/Event Co-ordinator.

Seminar II: Continuing Education For The Advanced Wedding Consultant

This seminar is restricted to Wedding Consultants/Event Co-ordinators who already have an established company or are with a related industry corporation. The advanced program includes, among other things, evaluation of your business plan, analysis of your profit/loss statement, industry trends, improving marketing, increased networking, creativity in wedding design, etc. Successful completion of Seminar II entitles participants to professional designation.

Professional Career Development Institute

The Professional Career Development Institute (PCDI) is a home study career school, based in Georgia, that has taught numerous courses to tens of thousands of people worldwide. All PCDI courses are accredited by the Accrediting Commission of the Distance Education and Training Council (which is recognized by the U.S. Department of Education). PCDI offers a thorough Bridal Consulting Career Diploma program.

Website: **www.pcdi-homestudy.com/courses/mr/**

Program: Bridal Consulting Career Diploma

Format: Correspondence program

Length: Work at your own pace. You should be able to complete the program between six months to one year and may be allowed up to two years to complete it.

Cost: $589 U.S. plus $24 shipping and handling

Contact: E-mail info@pcdi.com or phone 800-223-4542

The PCDI Bridal Consulting Diploma program includes 14 different lessons that will, amongst other things, show you how to build a bridal consulting business and market it. The program also covers lessons on etiquette, budgeting, time management, traditions, planning ceremonies and receptions, decorating, honeymoon planning, checklists, timelines and tables, etc. All books and materials are included in the cost.

Weddings Beautiful Worldwide

Weddings Beautiful Worldwide ("WBW") is a division of National Bridal Service ("NBS") for independent wedding consultants. NBS has been in business since 1951 and has a high standard of excellence. Membership in NBS includes nearly 800 stores and 4,000 wedding consultants throughout the world.

Website: **www.weddingsbeautiful.com/training.htm**

Program: Certified Wedding Specialist Program

Format: Correspondence program

Length: Completed at your own pace and schedule — on average it should take from six months to one year

Cost: $695 U.S. to receive all course materials at once or $100 to enroll and receive Assignment 1 and then $40 for each successive assignment for a total of $780

Contact: E-mail info@weddingsbeautiful.com or phone (804) 288-1220

WBW's Certified Wedding Specialist training program has 18 assignments and one test. The program aims to train you on all aspects of wedding co-ordinating and on having your own wedding co-ordinator business. Each assignment includes a questionnaire that is sent in to be graded and returned to the student with notes and/or corrections.

Some of the topics included in the eighteen assignments are: developing your business plan, developing wedding expertise, time management, directing various types of denominational and ethnic weddings, planning receptions, etc.

The Wedding Planning Institute

Lovegevity, a national wedding and event planning company, provides training and certification for wedding planners through their affiliated Wedding Planning Institute. One of their unique offerings is a "Fast-Track program" that gets you on your way to certification quickly. It can be completed from home, online or as a quick seminar.

Website: **www.weddingplanninginstitute.com**

Program: Wedding Planning Certification/Degree Programs

Format: Home study, online course, seminars, or individual classes

Length: You can take as little as eight weeks to complete the Fast Track course; the Degree program is based on 75 credit hours.

Cost: Start-up kit for any certification program is $99; self-study grading fee is $150. Online course fee is $595, Seminar fee is $495. For the degree program and individual classes, tuition is $125 per credit hour, and does not include the cost of books and materials.

Contact: E-mail admissions@weddingplanninginstitute.com or call 1-888-345-2898, Ext. 9000.

Topics of study include contracts, etiquette, flowers, music, day of services, marketing, running the business, etc. It is possible to register online. You can study the starter kit before you decide what format you want to take the course in, and Fast Track credits can be transferred to the degree program if you decide you want more intensive training.

3.4.3 Continuing Education Courses

Your local college or university may offer wedding planning or consulting courses. Through the continuing education department, you may be able to take a single course on a Saturday or over several evenings, and learn about planning a wedding, dealing with vendors or other wedding topics. Not only can this be a valuable learning experience, but you can also list any wedding planning courses you have taken on your resume or in a brochure that you provide to potential clients.

Phone local colleges and universities and ask for the continuing education department (or adult education). That department should be able to tell you if they offer a wedding/bridal consulting certificate or wedding consultant courses. In addition to colleges and universities, you may find courses or seminars in basic wedding planning offered by:

- Bridal or wedding consulting associations

- Local high schools

- Business colleges (check the Yellow Pages under "schools")

Following is a sample of some great seminars offered by two bridal consulting associations and one online educational institution.

The Association of Bridal Consultants

In addition to correspondence programs, the Association of Bridal Consultants also offers educational seminars and workshops. Seminars cover a variety of topics such as the role of the consultant, consulting with the bride, etiquette, marketing, business planning, fees and contracts, etc. The seminars are scheduled throughout the year at locations across the U.S. and are listed at the web address given below.

Website: **www.bridalassn.com/seminars.tmpl**

Programs: Seminars

Length: 1 day

Cost: Varies, but usually around $199 U.S. (includes a continental breakfast and course materials)

Contact: E-mail office@bridalassn.com or phone (860) 355-0464

Special Interest Courses

You may have heard the expression "A little learning is a dangerous thing." While having just a little knowledge on a variety of subjects may not be a good thing in other professions, this is definitely not true in the wedding industry. In fact, the more information and services you can offer your clients the better.

For instance, let's say you've just arrived at the reception venue and found that the florist did not accommodate the bride's wishes and included pink roses in the head table arrangements. Having taken a flower-arranging course, you are confident enough to jump right in and take out the offending colored flowers and rearrange the whole bunch before the bridal party even arrives.

Or, the bride and groom are trying to decide on an appropriate wine to serve at their home-hosted rehearsal dinner. With a little knowledge of wine and food pairings you are able to offer a couple of suggestions.

Useful special interest courses for planning weddings include:

- Flower arranging

- Wine tasting

- Arts and crafts courses geared to weddings

- Budgeting

- Balloon art

- Catering classes

- Cake Decorating

These classes are relatively inexpensive and you should be able to write off a portion of the tuition come tax time. (Check with your accountant before signing on the dotted line.) Look for these and other classes offered through your local college and university or adult education institutions.

4. Wedding Industry Jobs

Once you have developed your skills and knowledge of wedding planning, it's time to start getting paid for your talents!

As a wedding planner you have many exciting career possibilities which fall into one of two categories: (1) get a job in the wedding industry or (2) start your own wedding planning business. As you can see from the title, this chapter focuses on the first of these two options.

Job titles and specific duties vary depending on the employer. Common job titles for salaried positions are "bridal consultant" or "wedding co-ordinator." However, you may find wedding industry positions with a wide variety of titles, including customer service or sales associate.

4.1 Types of Employers

4.1.1 Resorts and Hotels

Resorts

One of the most fabulous jobs you can have in the wedding industry is working as a wedding co-ordinator at a luxury resort. A resort is any place that people visit for recreation or relaxation.

A position as a wedding co-ordinator at a resort can offer wonderful benefits including, in some cases, the opportunity to live and work in a tropical paradise. And with the tremendous growth in the number of "destination weddings" over the past few years (they now make up more than 10% of weddings), there is increased job security and more demand for wedding co-ordinators.

Popular wedding destinations for North American couples include:

- Banff, Alberta

- The Caribbean

- Colorado

- Disney World

- Europe (England, France, Greece, Ireland, Italy)

- Florida

- Hawaii

- Las Vegas

- Mexico

- New Orleans

- The Poconos (Pocono Mountains, PA)

Of course, there are many other popular destinations in addition to those listed above. For example, in the United States, couples choose to marry everywhere from New York to Palm Springs.

As a wedding co-ordinator, your job will involve handling arrangements for couples who will be coming from out of town to get married at your resort. In addition to the usual tasks involved in planning a wedding ceremony and reception (music, menus, flowers, photography, etc.), there may be a number of additional tasks, such as picking the couple up at the airport, helping them get a local marriage license, and finding someone to perform the ceremony. Depending on the facilities available at your resort, your job may also involve arranging recreational activities for the couple and their guests – from spa visits to golfing to a candlelit dinner for the newlyweds.

There are a number of large companies offering wedding packages at resorts. Wyndham Resorts offer weddings in destinations from Arizona to Aruba, Colorado to Key West, Mexico to Martha's Vineyard, and Disney World. You can find information about their destination wedding packages at their website at **www.destinationweddingsbywyndham.com**.

Other companies offering wedding packages at a number of different resort properties include Sandals Resorts (**www.sandals.com/general/ wedding.cfm**) and SuperClubs (**www.super-clubs.com/activities/ wedding/sc_wedding.asp**). Although their wedding packages are handled by other companies (contact information for which is available on either their webpages or by calling the applicable resort), many resorts offer a variety of wedding specials to choose from for couples getting married at their resort.

There are also many hotel chains with resort properties. Virtually every Caribbean resort offers wedding packages, as do resorts throughout the rest of the world. And, of course, it is not only resorts that are part of a large chain that offer wedding services.

Many locally owned properties offer packages for couples planning to tie the knot. For example, the Musket Cove Island Resort in Fiji advertises "our friendly wedding co-ordinator will be there to help you plan every detail of your special day" while the Hanalei Colony Resort in Hawaii has a full page about their wedding co-ordinator at **www.wedding-in-kauai.com/coordinator.html**.

One way to get hired as a wedding co-ordinator for a resort is to apply directly to the particular resort you want to work with. However, this method usually works well only if you live in the community where the resort is located. That's because there are usually local applicants who would be interested in the job, and a resort is not likely to have a job applicant fly in from out of town for an interview.

There may also be legal restrictions if the job is in a different country. For example, non-residents of Caribbean countries can only get a work permit from the relevant government if the job cannot be filled by a resident.

If you don't live in a resort community, and don't want to move there before you have a job lined up, you may possibly be able to work your way up to the job of your dreams by working with a resort or hotel chain. By working with a company that has a number of properties in different locations, you could start with a job in your own community then apply for a transfer to a resort location when a position opens up.

However, as there is no guarantee that a position at a resort will open up, or that you would be hired if such a position did open up, don't take this route unless you will be happy with the original job you apply for!

In the next section you will find links to a number of major hotel chains — many of which have resort properties.

Hotels

Many resort communities also have hotels with special packages for couples who are getting married. For example, in the Caribbean, wedding packages are offered by hotels such as the Radisson. However, you do not have to move to a resort community to start working with a hotel. Many cities (probably the city you live in now) have dozens of hotels with facilities for wedding receptions.

A hotel may be the site of many events — from banquets to business meetings to bar mitzvahs. Therefore, many hotels do not hire someone with the specific title of "wedding co-ordinator" because arranging wedding receptions is only part of the job.

If you want to work with a hotel, the department that will give you an opportunity to work with couples planning a wedding reception is the "sales and catering" department (at some hotels it may be known as just "sales" or just "catering").

A typical entry level position is "sales co-ordinator," a job that may involve more administrative work than actually working with customers. At some hotels, the next level up is "sales representative," or you may just move into the position of "sales manager" or "catering sales manager." At a single hotel, there may be several such positions. (The person at the top may have a title such as "director of catering services" or "director of sales and marketing.")

Someone who is at the sales manager or catering sales manager level may specialize in weddings. For example, at the Fairmont Waterfront Hotel in Vancouver, B.C., there are a couple of people who concentrate on booking weddings.

In addition to helping the couple make arrangements for their wedding reception, your job may involve assisting them with other parts of their wedding, for example, by referring them to vendors.

To find a job in the hotel industry, you can start by contacting hotel chains you are interested in working with. Major hotel chains list hotel locations for themselves and partner hotels at their websites so you can apply directly to the hotel(s) where you are interested in working. You may also find a few job opportunities listed online. Here are sites of luxury hotel chains. You can also find hotel links at **www.lhw.com**.

- *Fairmont Hotels and Resorts*
  www.fairmont.com

- *Hilton Hotels*
  www.hilton.com

- *Marriott International*
  www.marriott.com

- *Radisson Hotels*
  www.radisson.com

- *The Ritz-Carlton*
  www.ritzcarlton.com

- *Starwood Hotels (Sheraton, Westin)*
  www.starwood.com

You can find many hotels in your city simply by checking the Yellow Pages. As well as looking under "hotels," check under "weddings" to see if there are any ads from hotels that want to attract couples looking for a place to hold their wedding reception. Those hotels may be more likely to hire someone as a wedding co-ordinator, or at least they may give you a greater opportunity to work on wedding receptions.

Another way to find hotels is by checking with convention and visitors bureaus. The site **www.officialtravelguide.com** lets you do a search by city, and brings up a link for that city's convention and visitors bureau (C&VB). Click on the link to go to the official page for the C&VB and you can then click on either accommodations or hotels to search for facilities.

Don't limit yourself to hotels that are part of a large chain. An example of a local inn with a wedding co-ordinator on staff is Madrona Manor in Healdsburg, California. Visit **www.madronamanor.com/weddings.htm**.

4.1.2 Other Locations

Reception Venues

Any place a couple might choose to host a wedding reception is a possible place to apply for a job. Examples of venues where wedding receptions are held include:

- Chambers of commerce

- Convention centers

- Country clubs

- Golf clubs

- Yacht clubs

While some facilities may have a wedding co-ordinator on staff, others may hire sales and catering staff to book a variety of events, including weddings.

To find places to apply to, check the Yellow Pages under "clubs", "catering" or "weddings." If you can't find your local convention center in the phone book, simply type the name of your city and "convention center" or "conference center" into a search engine such as Google.com. To find chambers of commerce you can check the World Chamber of Commerce Directory at **www.chamberofcommerce.com**.

Attractions

Any place that attracts tourists (known as an "attraction") may offer a possible job opportunity for a wedding co-ordinator.

As mentioned in the section on resorts, among the most popular wedding destinations are Disneyland and Disney World. They hire wedding co-ordinators to help couples plan "fairytale weddings and honeymoons." You can read more about Disney's Fairytale Weddings and Honeymoons at **http://disney.go.com/vacations/disneyweddings**.

To find job openings at Disney, visit the Disney Careers webpage at **http://disney.go.com/disneycareers** or write to either of the two main Disney resorts in the U.S. If no wedding co-ordinator positions are available, you may want to consider applying for another position to get your foot in the door.

The Disneyland Resort
Professional Staffing
P.O. Box 3232
Anaheim, CA 92803-3232
Fax: (714) 781-1616

Walt Disney World Resort
P.O. Box 10090
Lake Buena Vista, FL 32830
Fax: (407) 828-1571

There are thousands of other attractions that can be the site of a wedding and/or reception. Most weddings held at an attraction are similar to weddings held at a church. However, some offer couples a unique wedding based on the theme of the attraction. You can read an article on theme weddings with plenty of links to creative ideas like skydiving and castles at **www.lovetripper.com/theme-weddings**.

The Internet is a great way to find attractions by checking websites of convention and visitors bureaus. At **www.OfficialTravelinfo.com** you can do a search by city to get a link for that city's convention and visitors bureau (C&VB). Click on the link to go to the official page for the C&VB and then click on attractions.

You can also do a search the good old fashioned way by checking out tourist information counters at hotels, visitors bureaus, and even your local airport for brochures on local attractions.

> **TIP:** If a popular attraction in your community doesn't offer a wedding package, you could approach them and suggest creating a new department with you as the wedding co-ordinator. Armed with the information on marketing that you will find in the next chapter of this guide, you might explain how you could help to promote the attraction to couples who are planning a wedding. If you can show how you will bring more revenue to the attraction than it will cost to employ you, you could create your own job! You will get tips on how to create your own job later in this chapter.

4.1.3 Retailers

Retail offers many job opportunities for those who want to work in the wedding industry and have the security of a steady paycheck. Most job openings are for entry-level or junior positions that will give you an opportunity to learn more about one or more areas of the wedding industry.

While hourly rates are typically low, many positions offer commissions which can add substantially to your income. For example, *The Los Angeles Times* reported in February 2002 that top consultants for a bridal store (David's Bridal) can earn $40 to $50 per hour in salary and commissions.

The main focus of a retail job is selling the store's merchandise by helping people choose products for the wedding. While most jobs with wedding retailers involve working with the bride (the job title is usually "bridal consultant"), a retail position may also include assisting others who are involved with the wedding, such as the groom, mother of the bride, attendants, and guests.

The job of a bridal consultant involves asking questions to find out the couple's preferences, color scheme, budget, etc. The bridal consultant will then recommend suitable products, and give the bride or others involved with the wedding information about the recommended products. Some positions also involve assisting the couple with other aspects of the wedding. Retailers that hire salespeople to work with brides and grooms include:

- bridal shops

- formal wear stores

- florists

- jewelry stores

- department stores

- other retailers with gift registries

Depending on your interests and goals, working as a bridal consultant/salesperson for any of these retailers may be a rewarding career in itself, or it may be a stepping-stone to another career in the wedding industry.

For example, if you stay in retail you may move into a position such as *buyer* (someone who decides what merchandise the store will carry) or *manager*. Or you might use what you learn during your retail experience to help you start your own wedding planning business.

Stores with Gift Registries

In case you are not familiar with bridal gift registries, they are a free service offered by many large retailers. Couples can register a list of gifts they would like to receive, then the guests invited to the wedding can refer to the list for assistance in choosing suitable wedding gifts. Not only is gift buying made easier for guests, registering makes it more likely the couple will receive gifts they really want and need.

Traditional gift registry items include china, crystal, linens, and silver, but couples may register anything else they want — from camping gear to art. Stores that offer gift registries include department stores, jewelry stores, housewares stores, and gift stores.

As a bridal consultant, your job would involve assisting couples in registering, with the aim of increasing sales for the store. A good example of what is involved in this job is explained in a job description for the position at Macy's. At Macy's the bridal consultant is expected to: "Guide couples through the registration process using advanced knowledge of home store merchandise, with specific attention to lifestyle and entertaining needs."

Macy's is only one of many retailers that hire bridal consultants to assist couples in registering for gifts. For your convenience, here is a list of some of the major retailers that offer bridal gift registries along with their website addresses. Many of these companies list store locations at their websites, and suggest that you apply directly to the store or stores where you are interested in working.

You may also find a few job opportunities listed online. For example, a recent visit to the Bloomingdale's site found four current job openings in the "Special Services - Bridal Consultant" department.

- *The Bay (Canada)*
  www.hbc.com/bay

- *Bloomingdale's*
  www.bloomingdales.com

- *BonMacy's (formerly The Bon Marché)*
  www.bonmacys.com

- *Crate & Barrel*
  www.crateandbarrel.com

- *Debenham's (Britain)*
  www.debenhams.com

- *Macy's*
  www.macys.com

- *Neiman Marcus*
  www.neimanmarcus.com/index.jhtml

- *Restoration Hardware*
  www.restorationhardware.com

- *Tiffany & Co.*
  www.tiffany.com

- *Williams-Sonoma*
  http://www.williams-sonoma.com

These are only a few of the many retailers that offer registries. For example, in different parts of the U.S., stores such as Burdines, Goldsmith's, Gump's, Lazarus, and Rich's, all have bridal registries. If this career opportunity interests you, the retailers to check with in your community include department stores, housewares stores (linens, kitchenware, etc.), and gift stores.

Bridal Shops

Bridal shops are stores that sell wedding gowns, dresses for bridesmaids, mothers, and flowergirls, as well as accessories such as headpieces, shoes, gloves, lingerie, hosiery, etc. Some bridal shops also provide additional services such as tuxedo rental and wedding invitations.

The number-one bridal retailer in the United States is David's Bridal, with more than 160 stores across the country. At the time this guide was written, the company had more than 100 recent job openings for bridal consultants, wedding consultants and other positions listed at **www. monster.com** (do a keyword search for "bridal"). There are thousands of smaller retailers throughout the country. You can find bridal shops in your community by checking your local Yellow Pages under "bridal shops."

If you are interested in working with grooms, expand your search to include "formal wear" or "tuxedo rentals" as well.

Florists

While most florists do not limit their business to weddings, employment with a florist may give you an opportunity to start working with quite a few brides. In addition to providing bouquets, many florists also provide decorations for the ceremony and reception. A few small florists have even branched out into providing complete wedding co-ordination services such as arranging for the caterer, music, photographer, etc.

Most cities have dozens of florists. To find them, check the Yellow Pages or see **www.floristlocators.com** (U.S.), **www.canadasflorists.com** (Canada), or **www.findflorist.co.uk** (U.K.).

4.1.4 Wedding Planners

An excellent way to work in the industry is by joining a company that already does wedding planning. As mentioned earlier in this guide, these companies and their owners may refer to themselves as any of the following (we use the term "wedding planner" to refer to all of them):

- Bridal consultants

- Wedding co-ordinators

- Wedding consultants

- Wedding planners

While you may be able to find a wedding planning company that is looking to hire full-time wedding planners, most positions involve working as an assistant to a wedding planner. (If you saw the movie *The Wedding Planner*, you will remember that Jennifer Lopez's character had an assistant.) As an assistant to a wedding planner, you may be involved with all aspects of the company's work.

A published job ad for an "Assistant Wedding Co-ordinator" included these job duties:

Responsible for generating new clientele by contacting brides to set up appointments, accompany consultant on appointments and assist with bridal shows, bridal showers and weddings. Other responsibilities include: assisting with bridal co-ordination, decorating, setup for bridal shows, favor making, etc.

As an assistant to a wedding planner you can learn a tremendous amount about the industry, which you may then be able to use in your own wedding planning business at some point in the future.

> **TIP:** When applying for jobs don't tell wedding planners you are looking for a job so you can get experience to start your own wedding planning company. Most business owners do not want to help train a potential competitor!

Finding Wedding Planners

You can find wedding planners online, in the Yellow Pages, or through word of mouth.

One place that lists wedding planners online is The Association of Bridal Consultants (ABC) website. If you click on "Association Members in Your Area" at **www.bridalassn.com** you may be able to find some firms that do wedding planning listed under "Co-ordinators/Bridal Consultants." However, because ABC members have to pay to be included in the list, not all members are included. Some states, such as California, have quite a few wedding planners listed while other states have none.

A site that lists wedding planners by state and country is the Open Directory Project. While the listings for some countries are small (for example, there are only 13 listed for all of Canada and 17 for Australia), there are more than 350 "wedding consultants and co-ordinators" listed in the United States. Visit **www.dmoz.org** and type in "wedding consultants."

By far the best place to search for local wedding planners is in the Yellow Pages under "weddings." If you check your local Yellow Pages listings, you will likely find a number of wedding planners (or wedding consultants, wedding co-ordinators, and bridal consultants) listed for your city.

Before you start applying for jobs, realize that most wedding planning companies are small businesses that manage to find just enough work for the company's owners. Because of this, it is usually not a productive use of your time to repeatedly phone every wedding planner in the Yellow Pages trying to find a job. Instead, if you are eager to work with a wedding planning company, you should focus your efforts on busy companies that are more likely to need extra staff to handle all the work they have coming their way.

These may be wedding planners that advertise a lot, or that you see mentioned in the local newspaper, see at bridal fairs, hear about through networking, or meet through information interviews. (All of these are covered elsewhere in this guide.)

4.1.5 Churches and Synagogues

A church or synagogue may hire someone to assist couples with preparing for the wedding ceremony. (The job does not involve assisting with the wedding reception.) The job title for this position is "wedding coordinator" and may involve:

- Co-ordinating bookings for the church or synagogue facilities

- Holding group orientation sessions for couples (e.g. once per month)

- Meeting with each couple to plan their ceremony

- Explaining church or synagogue policies affecting weddings (such as decorations that are acceptable, whether throwing rice is allowed, etc.)

- Advising couples on all aspects of the ceremony (such as seating, the processional, arrangements at the altar, etc.)

- Providing a list of resources such as musicians

- Answering questions by e-mail or phone

- Conducting the wedding rehearsal

- Supervising on the day of the ceremony

Here is a typical job description showing what a wedding co-ordinator does on the day of the ceremony:

> On the day of the wedding, the church wedding co-ordinator will arrive approximately one hour prior to the beginning of the wedding. He or she will supervise all pre-service arrangements and direct the entrance of the bride, wedding party, and seating of the families. After the ceremony is concluded and the wedding party is dismissed to the reception, the church wedding co-ordinator's responsibilities are complete.

Finding a Position

At some churches and synagogues, wedding co-ordinating is done by a full-time office administrator or administrative assistant as part of their job. At others, it is a volunteer position. In most cases, being a wedding co-ordinator is a part-time job, with payment per wedding (e.g. a $200 fee which is included in the amount paid by the couple for the use of the church).

The wedding co-ordinators we spoke with agreed that the best way to break into a wedding co-ordinator position is with a church or synagogue that you currently attend.

Whether or not a particular church or synagogue needs a wedding co-ordinator depends on the size of the congregation and the number of weddings held each year. For example, Christy Erion got her part-time home-based job as a wedding co-ordinator at Centre Street Church in Calgary, Alberta, after the congregation grew to 4,500 people, with about 60 weddings per year being held at the church.

If this is a position that interests you, and you happen to attend a growing church that doesn't yet have a wedding co-ordinator, you may be able to create a job for yourself helping couples prepare for their special day. (More information on creating your own job can be found later in this chapter.)

4.1.6 Wedding Vendors

As you saw earlier in this guide, there are many types of companies that provide services for weddings. These include:

- Bakers (wedding cakes)

- Beauty salons

- Caterers

- Concierge services

- Disc jockeys

- Limousine services

- Party supply companies

- Photographers

- Printers (invitations and stationery)

- Videographers

Most companies that offer the services listed above have many different types of clients. For example, a caterer may prepare meals for businesses or individuals planning dinner parties. A limousine service may provide cars for high school proms and dignitaries. A printer may print magazines and business cards in addition to invitations.

As a result, many of these companies do not have a wedding specialist on staff because weddings make up only part of their business. Nevertheless, if a particular company does any work with weddings, a job with them may give you a foot in the door.

Not only can you get experience working with couples planning their weddings, but you may be able to convince the company owner that there is enough potential business to put you in charge of a "wedding department." For example, an article about Changes Salon and Day Spa in Norfolk, Virginia, reported they have a Special Events/Wedding Co-ordinator on staff. (They had 82 employees at the time the article was written.)

You can find local services in the Yellow Pages. Since category listings may vary from one city to another, you may have to look under several different categories. For example, you might look under "rental equipment" to find party supply rental companies. Of course, make sure you also look under "weddings" because you will find companies that are especially interested in attracting wedding business.

4.2 Finding Job Openings

There are several places that wedding industry jobs may be advertised. If you're lucky, you may find a position in the classifieds of your local newspaper. However, as most jobs in this industry are not advertised in the classifieds, it will usually take more effort to find job openings.

4.2.1 Advertised Positions

Job Websites

Although there are no online job boards specializing in jobs for wedding planners, several job sites occasionally include postings for jobs in the wedding industry. For example, here's an excerpt from a Macy's ad previously posted at HotJobs.com (we searched under "bridal"):

BRIDAL MANAGER

As a Bridal Registry Manager, you will create new business and develop and train bridal consultants. While managing the entire bridal registry program for a specific location, you will interface with all levels of store management and outside vendors.

You will develop creative techniques to increase sales volume and the number of bridal registrations. This position leads to a Regional Bridal Manager position or to a career in Merchandising or Sales Support Management.

Websites that sometimes have listings for wedding industry jobs include those listed below. To see all possible jobs, do a search for "bridal" and a separate search for "wedding" (rather than searching for specific jobs titles such as "bridal consultant" or "wedding co-ordinator").

- *Careerbuilder.com*
  www.careerbuilder.com

- *HotJobs.com*
  http://hotjobs.yahoo.com

- *Monster.com*
  www.monster.com

At these websites, you can also search by type of employer. For example, if you are interested in working for a "resort," "hotel," "caterer," etc., you can search for that particular term. For example, the following ad turned up during a search at Monster.com for the keyword "caterer":

CATERING SALES REP / EVENT PLANNER

Catering by Windows, the Washington, D.C., area's premiere caterer, is known as one of North America's leading providers of exceptional food, cutting-edge culinary creativity and outstanding presentation. The company provides full service catering, party planning and event management to meet any catering need, from corporate receptions to weddings and fundraisers to backyard barbecues. Every affair begins with an experienced and attentive event consultant who custom designs each menu and co-ordinates food, décor and presentation to ensure a spectacular event.

If you are interested in the hospitality industry (resorts, hotels, caterers), there are a number of additional job sites you can check, including the following. However, these sites have relatively few listings compared to the major job sites listed above.

- *Hospitality Jobs Online*
  www.hospitalityonline.com

- *Hotel Jobs Network*
  www.hoteljobsnetwork.com/js/index.php

- *Hospitality 1st*
  www.hospitality-1st.com/Employers

Company Websites

Most companies advertise job openings at their websites. If there is no link for "jobs" or "careers" on the home page, click on the link for information about the company. That will usually take you to a page that includes a link to job postings.

Section 4.1 of the guide includes links to some major employers. You can find other large companies through Hoover's website at **www. hoovers.com**, which allows you to search by name or by industry. Hoover's directories are also available at many bookstores and libraries.

4.2.2 Unadvertised Positions

The *Harvard Business Review* is reported to have said that almost 80% of jobs are not advertised in the classifieds. That figure may be even higher for a fab job like wedding planner. In fact, it is rare to find ads placed by certain types of employers such as wedding planning firms.

Even among the types of employers that usually do advertise for bridal consultants or wedding co-ordinators, smaller companies may not have a website, and are unlikely to spend hundreds of dollars to post jobs at a site such as Monster.com. So how do these employers find employees?

Networking

Many employers find employees through word of mouth. When a small business owner needs a new employee, they will typically ask friends, business associates, and current employees if they know anyone who might be suitable for the job. In many cases, this is how they find the person for the job. An article at wetfeet.com estimates that 40 to 50% of jobs "are filled by candidates referred by staff members."

In the next chapter you will find practical advice on how to network to find clients. You can also use the advice in this part of the guide to help you meet and connect with people who can hire you – or recommend you to someone who can hire you – for a full-time or part-time job.

Direct Contact

Even if you don't know anyone connected to a particular company, it may still be possible to get a job there by contacting the company directly. It happens rarely, but sometimes a manager will have just made the decision that they need a new person, when they happen to receive a phone call or resume from someone who looks like they might be an ideal candidate for the job. Many employers would rather find someone this way than invest all the time and effort in advertising the job, screening resumes, and interviewing numerous candidates.

If you decide to make "cold" contact with employers (as opposed to the "warm" contacts that come through networking), it's a good idea to focus on specific types of employers. This will allow you to target your job search most effectively since it takes time to track down company owners' names, tailor your resume, and prepare personalized cover letters explaining why you want to work with that particular company.

4.2.3 How to Create a Job

Even when no job is open, someone may hire you if you can show them that you will give your employer more value than you cost. To do this, you will need to know what you can do for an employer that will outweigh the costs to the employer of hiring you. Here are some examples of things that employers see as "costs" when they hire a new employee:

- Your salary

- Your benefits

- Resources you'll need to do your job (e.g. computer, supplies)

- Time of other staff members to train you

- Time of your supervisor to oversee your work

As you can see, you will need to demonstrate to an employer that you would bring them more value than simply covering the cost of your salary. Here are some examples of what employers may see as valuable:

- Increasing profits by getting more sales

- Increasing profits by reducing the company's costs

- Freeing up your boss's time so they can do more important work

- Reducing your boss's frustration by doing tasks they don't like doing themselves

For example, a busy wedding planner might hire you to be their assistant if you can convince them that, with your help, they could do more of the tasks they enjoy and fewer of the tasks they don't enjoy, while being able to take on more weddings and earn more money.

Likewise, a company that occasionally provides services for weddings (such as a caterer, florist, party supply company, photographer, or resort) might hire you to set up a "wedding department" if you can convince them that you can increase profits by getting more customers. The next chapter offers many ideas on how to market your business and attract customers.

To create a job for yourself, you will need to deal directly with someone who has the authority to hire new people. This does not mean contacting the human resources (HR) department of a large company. The HR department fills positions that already exist. If you want to create a new position, you will need to speak with the appropriate department manager or, in the case of a smaller company, the owner of the company.

You will need to meet with this person and learn what they need to be able to figure out how you can create value for them. It's best if you can establish a relationship with someone through networking. However, you may even be able to create a job through cold calling. For example, here is the type of message you might leave on someone's voice mail:

Hello (name of potential employer), this is William Wedding. I am an experienced wedding co-ordinator, and would like to meet with you to discuss how I could help (insert name of potential employer's company) increase profits by having me market your company's services to brides. Please call me at (insert your phone number) so we can schedule a time to meet. (If you actually reach the person, simply change the last sentence to ask when would be a good time to meet.)

If the company is looking to increase profits, as many companies are, this call is more likely to get returned than a call simply asking if there are any job openings. You may need to be persistent and make a lot of calls, but if what you are offering is something that will bring a company more value than it costs, you can create a job!

4.3 Job Hunting Materials

4.3.1 Your Resume

Even if you have never been paid to plan a wedding, you can write a powerful resume that can help you get a job in the wedding industry.

In order to do this you will need to get some related experience using several of the methods suggested in chapter 3. Even if the only weddings you plan are for yourself, friends and family members, you will still have wedding planning experience! The key is to present that experience in a way that is attractive to employers.

Employers want to know you have the specific **skills** necessary to do the job they are hiring for. A resume containing too much irrelevant information could be rejected before the employer has even finished reading it. Therefore, instead of submitting a traditional resume focusing on each job you have ever held and what you did, create a **functional** resume focusing on the skills and experience the employer is looking for.

Exactly what you will include on your resume depends on both the job you are applying for and your previous experience. On the next page you will find a sample of a resume that could be used to apply for a position as an assistant to a wedding planner. If you are applying for a position with a retailer, make sure you include any previous retail jobs you have held. If you want to work with a resort, any experience in the hospitality industry would be an asset.

Sample Resume

Barbara Bridal
4321 Main Street
Sunnyday, California
Phone: (123) 555-1212
E-mail: bridal@abc.com

Objective

A position using my wedding planning, customer service and sales skills

Wedding Planning

- Consulted with brides and grooms to help them plan all aspects of their wedding
- Booked ceremony and reception sites
- Arranged for and supervised providers of flowers, music, catering, photography, video, limousines, and wedding stationery
- Decorated ceremony and reception sites (photos available on request)
- Assisted brides by addressing envelopes, arranging honeymoon travel, and running errands
- Served as wedding co-ordinator the day of the ceremony

Customer Service and Sales Representative

- Used effective listening skills to determine customer needs and recommend products
- Kept in touch with customers by telephone to ensure satisfaction
- Received thank-you letters from satisfied clients (available on request)
- As a sales representative, consistently exceeded sales targets by 20%

Work and Volunteer Experience

- Homemaker, 2001-2005
- Planned five weddings, 2004-2005
- Volunteer for Cancer Society, organizing fundraising events, 2002-2004
- Previous experience as an office assistant and salesperson for a women's clothing store

Education

- Successfully completed course on "Planning Your Wedding" at Sunnyday College Continuing Education, 2004

In fact, the following types of experience may be helpful for almost any types of jobs in the wedding industry:

- Sales

- Customer service

- Wedding planning

Something else to keep in mind is that you are applying for a job where appearances count. Choose an attractive paper stock, lay it out nicely on the page, and make sure there are no typos. Ask someone else to look it over before you send it out. Other basic principles of preparing an effective resume are the same as for any job. For example:

- Try to keep your resume to a single page unless you have extensive relevant experience.

- Do not go back further than 10 years — some employers may judge what you learned before then to be outdated.

- Your objective should be relevant to the position instead of a vague statement.

- Include all relevant education especially a degree or certification received.

- List accomplishments, such as awards, promotions and achievements as well as duties for each position.

- Do not include references on your resume, but have a list ready in case you are asked to provide it. Don't forget to get permission from the people you plan on using and only include them if you are absolutely certain their comments will be positive.

4.3.2 Cover Letter

If you are submitting your resume by mail, fax, or e-mail, it is recommended that you include a cover letter. While it's okay to photocopy your resume, your cover letter should be personalized, and explain why you are a good candidate for the job.

To see what to do – and what not to do – in a cover letter, we have included two sample letters prepared in response to this ad:

WEDDING CO-ORDINATOR

Royal Resort is seeking a wedding co-ordinator to help couples plan their wedding ceremony, reception and honeymoon at our resort. If you have previous wedding planning experience, along with strong customer service skills, please apply to _____.

In the cover letter below, Andy has done a number of things wrong. See how many of these mistakes you noticed:

- **The letter is addressed to "Dear Sirs."** Andy could make a better impression by addressing it by name to the person who will be reviewing resumes. If you don't know who to send your letter to, you can phone to ask the Human Resources department or address your letter "Attention: Human Resources." Since the person reading your letter may be a woman, avoid saying "Dear Sirs."

- **It doesn't say which position is being applied for.** Many companies advertise more than one position at a time.

- **It has typographical and grammatical errors** (e.g., confusing "you're" with "your"). Letters should be proofread before being sent.

- **The letter focuses on what Andy wants** (to enjoy the job and get experience), instead of what the company wants. Employers want to know what value you will bring to them.

Sample Cover Letter 1

Dear Sirs:

I saw you're ad. This is the kind of job I've been looking for. I'm pretty sure I would enjoy it and it would be good experience for me. I've already sent out a bunch of resumes without much luck so I hope you'll hire me. As you can see I have everything your looking for. Its your loss if you don't hire me. Call 5555-1212.

Andy Applicant

- **The letter doesn't mention the company by name.** Andy could make a much better impression by doing a little research in order to say something flattering about the company. (You can find out what companies pride themselves on by checking their websites.)

- By saying "I've already sent out a bunch of resumes without much luck" and "I hope you'll hire me," **Andy sounds desperate**. Employers may wonder if there's a good reason why no one else has hired Andy.

- As you can imagine, saying something like "It's your loss if you don't hire me" does not make a good impression!

Employers would be more impressed with this letter:

Sample Cover Letter 2

Attention: Terry Smith

I am writing to apply for the Wedding Co-ordinator position advertised in the *Saturday News*.

Royal Resort needs someone who has previous wedding planning experience and strong customer service skills. As my resume shows, I can bring you experience with assisting people to plan their wedding ceremony, reception, and honeymoon. I work to get repeat business for my employer, and have numerous letters from satisfied customers.

It would be an honor to work with our city's #1 resort. I would like to arrange a meeting to discuss how I can be of service to Royal Resort and your guests. Please call me at 555-1212 to arrange a meeting at your convenience. I look forward to hearing from you and working with you.

Andy Applicant

Your own cover letter will of course depend on the position you are applying for, and the company you are applying to. It should also include your name and contact information at the top of the page.

4.4 Interviews

Interviews for wedding industry jobs are much like interviews for other jobs. With that in mind, there are several specific tips that can help you make an excellent impression in an interview.

4.4.1 What Employers Are Looking For

Employers are looking for someone who will do a good job. But they are also seeking someone with a positive attitude and excellent interpersonal skills. Here is how some employers have described what they are looking for:

Bridal Shop: *"The qualified individual will have an up-beat attitude with excellent customer service skills."*

Catering Company: *"A great attitude is our #1 requirement."*

Resort: *"Strong customer service attitude is a MUST."*

Formalwear Store: *"The most important quality you need is a sincere love of working with people."*

What employers look for are specific behaviors demonstrating that you are the type of person who will work well with customers such as the bride and groom, their parents, members of the wedding party, or wedding guests. Many employers want to hire someone who is friendly, helpful, a good listener, and treats people with respect.

Your attitude and ability to get along with people are being judged from the moment you first walk into the place where you will be interviewed (or even earlier, when you first speak on the telephone with anyone from the company). Anyone you encounter in the lobby, the elevator, the washroom, or the reception area (if they have one) may have input into whether or not you are hired.

One of the authors of this guide has conducted hundreds of employment interviews, and routinely asks the receptionist about the person who had just been interviewed to find out if the applicant treated the receptionist with friendliness and respect.

During the interview itself, try to be as outgoing and enthusiastic as possible. Of course this isn't always easy because interviews can make people nervous, and nervous people tend to smile less, and act more stiff and formal than they normally would. However, in the wedding industry you will be constantly working with many new people. The employer wants to see that you are comfortable even in a potentially uncomfortable interpersonal situation such as an interview.

If you tend to be stiff and uncomfortable during an interview, it is time to perform. Act how you would if you did not feel nervous. This may feel unnatural at first, but behaving as if you are not nervous can actually make you start to feel more confident. It can also be very helpful to do some role plays (practice interviews) with a friend before you go to the interview.

As well as being enthusiastic, be positive. Avoid saying anything negative, especially about former employers. Focus on what value you would bring to the company as an employee, and not on what you want to get from the job. For example, don't discuss how much vacation time you want or bring up salary until the employer does.

Also avoid saying anything negative about yourself, which some applicants do by sounding as if they are desperate for a job. Before the interview remind yourself how much you have to offer an employer, and that there are many opportunities for you. Believe that if this particular job doesn't work out, there is something better out there for you.

Within 24 hours after the interview, write a thank-you letter to the person who interviewed you and anyone else who may have been helpful to you, such as the interviewer's assistant. Thank the interviewer for their time, give any additional information that you feel will help you get the job, and say how enthusiastic you are about the possibility of working with their company. You can send a thank-you letter by e-mail, but you will make an even better impression if you deliver it in person.

You want the interviewer and the other people you meet to think: "What a nice person! It would be great to have someone like that working here."

What to Wear

Because your job will involve dealing with couples who are planning a formal occasion, it's not surprising that many interviewers will consider your appearance, as well as your personality, when deciding whether or not you are a suitable candidate for the job. To make a good impression, you should be well groomed and professionally dressed.

If possible, visit the business before the interview so you can see how people are dressed. If that's not possible, ask the assistant of the person you are going to meet with about the company's dress code. If you have no information to go on, choose standard interview attire, such as a navy suit. (You can find some good tips on dressing professionally in section 5.4.2 on client consultations.)

4.4.2 Questions to Expect

You can expect to be asked standard interview questions such as the following so it's a good idea to prepare some answers before the interview.

- Why do you want to work for our company?

- What are you doing now?

- What kind of position are you looking for?

- What did you like most about your last job? What did you like least? Why?

- What experience do you have with _____? (Depending on the company, they may want to know your experience with wedding planning, selling, customer service, juggling several projects at once, etc.)

- What are your strengths? What are your weaknesses?

- What do you want to be doing in five years?

- What are your salary expectations?

- Do you have any questions for us?

In order to ask good questions and give an effective answer to "Why do you want to work here?" you will need to learn something about the company before the interview. Make sure you visit and read through their website, if they have one, or stop by the office to pick up any promotional brochures.

Also be prepared to answer behavioral questions. These are questions that ask you about an experience you had in the past, and require you to answer with a specific real-life example. The interviewer might say: "Tell me about a time you had to deal with a difficult customer. What happened, and how was it resolved?"

The interviewer will not be satisfied with a hypothetical answer about what you "would" do in such a situation. They want to hear about an actual time you dealt with a difficult customer. The purpose is not to see if you have ever had a difficult customer (they expect you have), the purpose is to see how well you resolve difficult situations. If something did not work out in the past, they want to know what you learned from it.

There is a wealth of information on interviewing techniques available through the Internet and/or your local library or bookstore. One such website is Monster.com, where you can find some more advice on preparing for an interview and answering standard interview questions at **http://interview.monster.com**.

4.4.3 Discussing Salary

If an employer is interested in hiring you, they will bring up the issue of salary. (As mentioned above, you should not be the first one to bring up salary if you want to make a good impression on the interviewer.)

To maximize your salary, try to get the employer to state a figure first. If you are the first one to mention a specific salary figure, and it's lower than the one the employer had in mind, you risk getting hired for less than they might have been willing to pay you. Therefore, if they ask your salary expectations, try turning the question back to them by saying something like "It depends on exactly what I would be doing. What is the salary range for this position?"

It's a good idea to have a sense of how much you should be getting paid before the issue comes up during an interview. The salary for the job may have been advertised. If not, there are a few ways to get a sense of a reasonable salary for the position. One possibility is to check out other job ads through the links provided earlier in this chapter to see if a salary range is listed. For example, an ad posted at Monster.com for a "Catering Manager/Wedding Specialist" at the Fairmont Hotel in Kansas City listed the salary as $30,000 – $40,000 U.S.

Another source of information about some types of salaries is **Salary.com**. For example, they state that a typical retail salesperson working in the United States is expected to earn a median base annual salary of $23,588. In addition to a base salary, retail salespeople may earn a commission. For example, a bridal shop that pays $8.00 per hour may offer a commission of 8% on sales, which could greatly increase your earnings. Be sure to ask the employer about average commissions if that will be part of your pay.

Salary.com also lists the median base salary in the United States for the wedding co-ordinator of a casino as $26,257 per year. They currently do not list salary information for other types of wedding planners. Salaries also vary widely depending on geographic area and type of employer. For example, a job with a small wedding planning firm in North Dakota will pay you less than a job with a large hotel in New York City. To get information about typical salaries in your community, connect with people in the wedding industry using the techniques described in this guide, such as informational interviews, mentoring, and networking.

In many cases, you may be able to negotiate a better salary or better benefits than the employer's initial offer. If the employer isn't flexible on salary, they may be able to offer higher commissions, or be willing to negotiate vacation or overtime.

In an article titled "Mastering the Art of Salary Negotiation" at the **CareerBuilder.com** website, James Powell says if the salary offer is low you should "discuss a 60, 90 or 120-day performance review and negotiate a potential minimum percentage increase" or ask about a year-end or signing bonus.

While effective negotiations can lead to a higher salary, if you really want an unlimited potential for income, then you should consider being self-employed. In the next chapter you will learn how to start your own wedding planning business.

5. Starting Your Own Business

As a self-employed wedding planner you can enjoy freedom and the potential for much higher income than you might earn as an employee. If you dream of having your own wedding planning business, the information in this chapter will help you get started and make your business a success. It covers:

- What you need to get started

- How to set up your office

- How much to charge for your services

- How to market your business

- How to get clients

When you finish this chapter you will know what needs to be done to start a wedding planning business, and have practical advice so you can go out and do it!

5.1 Getting Started

Before you can get to the fun part of having your own wedding planning business (planning weddings!) there are a number of not so fun, but very important, matters to be handled . Here are some good resources to help you as you start your business:

- *SCORE*
  The Service Corps Of Retired Executives has volunteers through-out the U.S. who donate time to mentor small businesses free of charge. Visit their website for helpful information or call 1-800-634-0245 to find the nearest SCORE counseling location.
  www.score.org

- *Small Business Administration*
  The SBA is an excellent source of free information for anyone starting a business in the U.S. To learn about SBA business development programs and services, call the SBA Small Business Answer Desk at 1-800-U-ASK-SBA (827-5722) or visit their website.
  www.sbaonline.sba.gov

- *ChamberBiz*
  The U.S. Chamber of Commerce website offers free information on preparing a business plan, incorporating, choosing your office location, and other aspects of starting and running a business. Phone (800) 638-6582 or visit their website.
  www.uschamber.com/sb

- *Online Small Business Workshop*
  The Canadian government offers an Online Small Business Work-shop which includes information about taxes, financing, incorpora-tion, and other topics.
  www.cbsc.org/osbw

- *Nolo.com Small Business Legal Encyclopedia*
  Nolo is a publisher of plain English legal information, books, soft-ware, forms and a comprehensive website. Their website also of-fers free advice on a variety of other small business matters. Their products are available in bookstores across the U.S.
  www.nolo.com/lawcenter/ency/index.cfm

5.1.1 Creating a Business Plan

Have you ever used a road map when driving someplace you hadn't been before? If so, you know that mapping out your route in advance can help you get to your destination more quickly and avoid getting lost. In many ways, creating a business plan can do the same for your business. Business planning involves putting on paper all the plans you have for your business, including:

- The services you will provide

- Who your clients are

- Who your competitors are

- Where you will find suppliers (vendors)

- What you will charge for your services

- How you will advertise and market your services

- How much money you will need to get started

If you enjoy being spontaneous, you may be thinking you'd prefer not to do much advance planning. However, if you are seeking financing for your business from a bank or other lender, they will expect to see a business plan that shows you have a viable business idea with an excellent chance for success. Even if you don't need financing, putting ideas on paper will give you the "road map" of where you want to go with your business and how you are going to get there.

A business plan can also help you avoid costly surprises. If you are considering whether to leave a secure job to start your own business, a business plan can help you determine the resources you will need to start your business and decide when the timing is best for you to get started.

While you are working on your business plan, you may start to question some of your previous ideas. You may come up with ideas that are even better, or decide to make some changes to ensure you have a greater chance of success.

Your Services and Customers

For wedding planners, a key component of your business plan will be deciding what services your business will offer, and who you will offer them to. When you are just starting out you may be tempted to say "I will do anything related to weddings that anyone will pay me to do!" A can-do attitude is wonderful to have, however, you may find you are able to attract more clients by offering specific services. For example, you could offer any – or all – of the following services:

Full Service Wedding Planning

A full service wedding planner is involved in all aspects of planning and co-ordinating the wedding ceremony and reception. As you saw in chapter 2, the tasks you may be responsible for range from budgeting and scheduling, to finding and negotiating with vendors. You will be in regular contact with your clients as the wedding approaches. In addition to planning before the wedding, you will be available throughout the entire event to assist with any last-minute details that arise.

Wedding Day Co-ordination

For couples who wish to plan their own weddings, you could offer your services as a wedding day co-ordinator. This allows the couple to enjoy their special day without the stress of overseeing all the vendors and activities. Most wedding day co-ordinators also co-ordinate the rehearsal. In fact, wedding co-ordinators typically start working with a couple about a month before the wedding so they can review what needs to be done, contact vendors, and develop a plan for the rehearsal and wedding day.

Wedding Consultations

For couples who want to do everything themselves – but want to know how to do it as easily and cost-effectively as possible – you can offer brief consultations to help them get started. For example, you might offer an hourly consultation (most planners suggest a two hour minimum) to help them plan a schedule, recommend specific vendors, prepare a preliminary budget, and answer any questions they may have.

A Special Case: Gay Weddings

Despite the flurry of recent media attention to gay marriage, same-sex couples have been holding commitment ceremonies for years. That means the market for planning weddings and other special events for gay, lesbian, and transgendered clientele has been around for some time.

In that community, the term gay wedding has gained increasing currency. "Anybody can have a wedding, and same-sex couples have been celebrating weddings for a long time," says Jenny Pizer, senior attorney at the western regional office of Lambda, an organization advocating full civil rights for gay, lesbian, bisexual, and transgendered individuals.

Pizer cites the legal difference between a *wedding*, which is a celebration and party, and *marriage*, and notes that the legal arena is changing very quickly. There are only two cases in which the ceremony itself could bring legal trouble: (1) for members of the military, which has rules against declaring oneself party to a same-sex union, and (2) for individuals whose immigration status is uncertain.

Your best resource for up-to-date information on the legal status of same-sex couples is the gay-advocacy community. In addition to various local groups that may be available in your area, such organizations as Lambda (**www.lambda.org**) and GLAAD (**www.glaad.org**) engage in vigorous outreach and have regional offices around the country. They track trends in culture and the law that have implications for their constituency and post them on their Internet sites.

As a wedding planner you work with a number of different vendors. When planning for this market segment, says Rita Leonard, co-owner with Paula Rutledge of Pride Bride (**www.pride bride.com**), a Winnipeg-based online resource for same-sex couples: "It's very important everybody that you list is completely *on side*, knowing that gay people are going to come to them." According to Leonard, there's still a considerable amount of social backlash regarding same-sex relationships.

Leonard says that vendors must have an absolute commitment to providing services for same-sex couples if everyone involved is to be satisfied. "It's a double bonus for us if the company is gay-owned," she says. She recommends that planners access websites to get a sense of whether a vendor is likely to be gay friendly, watching for the way the company in question uses language to describe services and clientele.

If you want business from the homosexual market segment, it is imperative to develop reliable sources of supply for such items as gay and lesbian wedding invitations, gifts and registries, cakes, vows, honeymoons, and even little details like cake toppers.

Venues are equally important. Banquet managers, top hotel officers, and all other venue staffers must be 100% pleased for gay couples to be there. Everyone must be informed. As Leonard explains, it could be very embarrassing for guests or staff to have to answer questions in the middle of an event.

A lot of gay weddings are planned and executed at one geographical remove. Most of Pride Bride's business, for instance, doesn't come from local sources or from major metropolitan areas but from smaller towns where there is little or no gay community and where the concept of a commitment ceremony is an alien idea.

For more than 25 years, East Coast Yacht Charters (**www.East CoastYachtChartersinc.com**) has run some 400 luxury yachts for hosting catered affairs, including weddings, in New York, New Jersey, Connecticut, Florida, and the Caribbean. "In the past, we had maybe two or three gay wedding inquiries per year," reports East Coast's Tom Gross. "That's risen to five or six per week."

Be on the lookout for information resources as the market for gay weddings evolves. St. Martin's Press has reportedly scheduled publication of *The Survival Guide to Gay Weddings* for 2005, and gay-wedding expos have been slated for Las Vegas, Boston, and San Francisco. See **www.gayweddingplanners. com** and **http://rainbowweddingnetwork.com** for more information.

Destination Weddings

Some wedding planners have built successful businesses by offering destination wedding services. A "destination wedding" is a wedding at a location such as a resort that the couple has to travel to. It may involve only the couple (commonly known as eloping) or it may also involve guests. An estimated 10% of weddings are destination weddings.

If you have travel industry experience, you might consider planning destination weddings at locations around the world. Some self-employed wedding planners even specialize in planning weddings on cruise ships.

Of course you would need to establish relationships with the appropriate vendors, such as cruise lines, in order to offer these kinds of services. (You can find information about working with vendors in section 2.6.) Examples of destination wedding sites include **www.moonrings.com** and **www.fantasiaweddings.com**.

For most wedding planners, the easiest way to offer destination wedding services is by arranging packages for couples who want to travel to your own community to get married. Obviously there will be a much bigger market for these services if you happen to live in a popular destination such as Hawaii. However, virtually any community that attracts tourists might be a possible wedding destination.

Examples of websites of wedding planners who specialize in organizing weddings for couples traveling to their communities include: **www. firstclassweddings.com** (Hawaii), **www.italianwedding.com** (Italy), and **www.weddingsonmackinac.com** (Michigan).

Vendor

Some wedding planners also offer related products and services such as catering, flowers, or wedding invitations. For example, if you have a talent for baking, you might make the wedding cakes for clients yourself rather than recommending another vendor.

If you want to offer services beyond wedding planning, you will need to do additional research about starting that type of business. The resources provided in the previous section may be helpful in pointing you in the right direction.

Other Parts of Your Plan

The other parts of a business plan (such as how much you will charge and how you will market your services to clients) are covered later in this chapter. As you read through those sections, make notes of what you would like to do with your own business.

As previously mentioned, the SBA offers an extensive selection of information on most business management topics. Online, they offer "Business Plan Basics" at **www.sba.gov/starting_business/planning/basic.html**.

This information is also available in print form in the "Resource Directory for Small Business Management." For a free copy, contact the nearest SBA office, which you can find listed in the U.S. Government section of your telephone directory.

5.1.2 Choosing a Business Name

Your business name can instantly communicate a powerful message to potential customers, so it should be memorable and easy to pronounce.

To choose a name for your wedding planning company, start by taking a look in the phone book or on the Internet to see the names that other wedding planners have chosen. Notice which names stand out. Your name might be creative, or you might choose a name that clearly communicates what your company does.

For example, in California some creative company names include "An Affaire of the Heart" and "engaging events," while straightforward company names include "Every Last Detail Wedding & Event Co-ordination," "Weddings by Design" and "The Wedding Experts."

For good advice on what to consider when choosing a business name visit the Nolo.com website or look for the Nolo publications as mentioned at the start of this chapter.

In most jurisdictions, if you operate under anything other than your own name, you are required to file for a fictitious name. It's usually just a short form to fill out and a small filing fee that you pay to your state or provincial government.

Before registering a fictitious name, you will need to make sure it does not belong to anyone else. If someone else has trademarked the name you are using, you may be forced to stop using the name and possibly have to pay the owner damages.

Search the federal trademark database to determine whether a name has already been registered with the U.S. Patent and Trademark Office (PTO). You can go to the PTO's Trademark Electronic Business Center and do a search.

U.S. Patent and Trademark Office
Mail Stop USPTO Contact Center
P.O. Box 1450
Alexandria, VA 22313-1450
Phone: 1-800-786-9199 or (703) 308-4357
Website: **www.uspto.gov/main/trademarks.htm** (choose "Search")

Canadians can find information and search a database of existing trade-marks through the Canadian Intellectual Property Office.

Canadian Intellectual Property Office (CIPO)
Place du Portage I
50 Victoria Street, Room C-114
Gatineau, Quebec K1A 0C9
Phone: (819) 997-1936
Website: **http://strategis.ic.gc.ca/sc_mrksv/cipo**

Most small businesses do not bother to trademark their names because it can be costly and time-consuming. However, if your company name is truly unique, you might want to consider it. You can try doing it yourself, or hire a lawyer specializing in "intellectual property" to do it for you.

5.1.3 Legal Matters

Your Business Legal Structure

Your business structure affects the cost of starting your business, your taxes, and your liability (responsibility) for any debts of the business. There are several different legal forms a business can have.

Sole Proprietorship

If you want to run the business yourself, without incorporating, your business will be known as a "sole proprietorship." This is the least expensive way to start a business. It is also the easiest because it requires less paperwork and you can report your business income on your personal tax return. One drawback to this type of business is that you are personally liable for any debts of the business.

Partnership

If you want to go into business with someone else, the easiest and least expensive way to do this is by forming a partnership. Legally, you would both be responsible for any debts of the company.

Working with a Partner

Beyond any legal issues, before going into business with a partner you should spend many hours talking about how you will work together, including:

- What each of you will be responsible for

- How you will make decisions on a day-to-day basis

- What percentage of the business each of you will own

- How you see the business developing in the future

- What you expect from each other

During your discussions you can learn if there are any areas where you need to compromise. For example, one of you may want to have a wedding planning business as a fun part-time job, while the other wants to work full-time and eventually build a business that will employ other people. You can avoid future misunderstandings by putting the points you have agreed on into a written "partnership agreement" that covers any possibility you can think of (including one of you leaving the business in the future).

Corporation

Whether you are working alone or with partners, if you want a more formal legal structure for your business, you can incorporate. Incorporation can protect you from personal liability and may make your business appear more professional to some clients.

However, it usually costs several hundred dollars and there are many rules and regulations involved with this type of business structure (among other requirements, corporations must file articles of incorporation, hold regular meetings, and keep records of those meetings). Many new business owners consult with an attorney before incorporating.

Limited Liability Company

A Limited Liability Company is a new type of business legal structure in the U.S. It is a combination of a partnership and corporation, and is considered to have some of the best attributes of both, including limited personal liability.

The resources at the start of this chapter have further information on business structures. Excellent advice is also offered at the Quicken website at **www.quicken.com/small_business/start**.

Business Licenses

You can find information about getting a city business license from your city hall. You may also be required to have a county or state license so be sure to check with regulatory agencies in your area to determine what you'll need. Check the resources mentioned in the first part of this section, or see the SBA's webpage at **www.sba.gov/hotlist/license.html**.

5.1.4 Taxes

You may be wondering why you need to think about taxes when you are just starting up your business. Certainly you don't have to pay taxes until you start making money. However, it may be advantageous to register with the government as soon as you can, and it is wise to plan ahead.

Tax Returns

If your business is a sole proprietorship or partnership in the United States, you will file a schedule C with your personal tax returns. You'll also have to file a form to determine the amount you owe on your social security.

When you fill out your tax return, you will need to include either your Social Security Number or an Employer Identification Number (EIN). A number of business owners recommend filling out an SS-4 Form to obtain an EIN even if your business is a sole proprietorship. Your corporate clients will need this for their records as will your suppliers to set up wholesale accounts. An EIN is also required if your company is incorporated, if you have employees, or if you plan to sell products (e.g. wedding invitations, wedding cakes, decorations, etc.)

Taxes on Product Sales

If you buy wedding supplies at wholesale prices then resell them to your clients for a higher price, you will need to collect sales tax from your clients and turn it over to the appropriate city, county, state, and/or country. In order to collect sales tax, you must be registered with, or have a sales tax license from, each level of government you collect taxes for.

> **TIP:** You do not need to obtain a sales tax license if your clients simply reimburse you the actual purchase price for any materials you buy for them.

To find out which taxes apply in your jurisdiction, check the resources below and consult with an accountant.

Resources

For tax information, forms and publications, see the resources at the start of this chapter or contact your government tax authority. Check your local phone directory for an office near you, call their national office, or visit their website.

The U.S. Internal Revenue Service (IRS) can be reached at (800) 829-4933 or online at **www.irs.gov**. In Canada, you can get information from the Canada Revenue Agency at (800) 959-5525 or online at **www.cra-arc.gc.ca/menu-e.html**.

5.2 Setting Up Your Business

To help get your business up and running, this section offers advice on:

- Location
- Telephone
- Equipment and supplies
- Insurance
- Employees
- Finances

5.2.1 Location

The first thing you will need is a place to work. Your choices include working from home or renting space. Many wedding planners choose to work from home when they start their businesses, because it saves on the cost of an office.

Identify Your Needs

Although clients may not come to your office very often, you will need to ensure you have enough space to carry out your business. Ask yourself if you will need any of the following. (If you're not sure, you can make a mental note and return to this section after you have read through the entire guide.)

- Storage space for materials or supplies
- Space for assembly (e.g. of decorations)
- Space for employees

Working from Home

There are many benefits to working from home. For example, you don't have to commute to an office, you can take breaks whenever you want, you can spend more time with your family, etc.

Another important benefit is that you are allowed to deduct from your income tax a percentage of your mortgage interest and property tax (or your rent) along with a similar share of some utilities and maintenance. See the section on taxes to find out where to get information and forms for business deductions.

If office space is expensive in your area and you have enough room to work from home, your financial breaks can really add up. But first, make sure your local zoning laws allow you to have a home-based business in your neighborhood. Zoning laws are often regulated by a city or county's planning department. To contact the department, look up "zoning" or "planning" in the government section of your phone book.

To help you focus on business, and keep other family members from intruding on your workspace, try to find at least an entire room to use for your office. (Having a separate room also makes it easier to calculate your tax deduction.) You could work from a spare bedroom, a den, a basement, or any other area that can be kept separate from the rest of the house.

Set regular office hours when the rest of the family knows you're working and not to be interrupted unless there's an emergency. (And train your family to know what you mean by "emergency" — a house on fire is an emergency; needing to know where the cookies are is not).

Once you have chosen your space, decorate it beautifully because you may have clients dropping by. Plus, it's tax deductible! (Remember to make your workspace functional with as large a desktop as possible, and a comfortable chair.)

Renting Space

While a home office works well for many wedding planners, others prefer to rent a separate space. If you find it challenging to stay motivated, or tend to get easily distracted when you're at home, an office may be just what you need to help you focus on business.

A separate space also creates a better impression if you plan to have people visit you. If you want a place to meet with clients and vendors, or work with employees, you might want to consider getting an office outside your home.

Look for a place that is convenient to get to from your home, and that gives you quick access to any services you may need. Such services might include your bank, suppliers of materials, even a good coffee shop! Pick an area that suits your needs and fits your budget. For good advice on what to consider before renting space check out the resources mentioned at the start of this chapter.

5.2.2 Telephones

You'll notice this section is titled "Telephones" rather than simply "Telephone." That's because many wedding planners have more than one phone. For many business owners, the basics are a business line, a fax line, and a cell phone.

If you are on the Internet a lot sending e-mails to clients, or searching for ideas, you may want to invest in a high-speed Internet connection, cable connection or satellite connection, where available. Dial-up Internet access not only busies your phone line, but it is not capable of handling the large attachments common in e-mails today. If dial-up is all that you have available, get a separate line to connect to the Internet so at least your phone calls can get through.

If you have employees, you may want phone lines for them as well. Here is some information to help you decide what is best for you — and how to best use the lines you have.

Your Business Line

A true business line will cost a little more than a residential line but you will be listed under your business name in the white pages and under directory assistance (which makes it easy for clients to find you) and you can receive a free listing in the Yellow Pages under "Weddings."

If you work at home, it's a good idea to have a separate telephone line that is off limits to the rest of the family. Your telephone should always be answered professionally with the name of your business. You will find helpful advice on what to say during your first telephone conversation with a bride-to-be in section 5.4. If you want to ensure your phone is answered at all times during business hours, you can hire someone to answer it for you.

TIP: Don't hire an answering service that only takes messages. These are services that say in response to callers' questions: "I don't know, I'm just the answering service." This is frustrating to callers and can create a poor impression.

If you decide to use someone to answer your calls, it is better to hire an individual, possibly working from home, who can answer callers' questions and act as a public relations person for you. See the information below for hiring employees.

A less expensive option to hiring someone to answer your calls is to use voice mail. Voice mail is widely accepted in business communication. For example, if you call the direct line of a corporate executive, you will probably get voice mail if you don't connect with the executive. If you do opt for voice mail, consider leaving your pager or cell phone number for callers who may have an urgent need to reach you.

Additional Phones

Your Internet connection can double as a fax machine with software such as Windows' built-in fax software or a product like Winfax Pro. Even if your voice mail comes on while you're on the phone, it's wise to have a separate line for faxes. A potential client may not be impressed to hear you say, "Please wait a few minutes before sending that fax because I have to switch on the machine." (It suggests you are just a beginner working from home.)

If there will be more than one person in the office or if you expect a moderate to heavy amount of incoming calls, you should consider buying a two-line phone and getting a roll-over line. Your local phone company can set up the service.

A cell phone is not optional in this business. As a successful wedding planner, you can expect to spend a lot of time away from your office visiting clients in their homes and at other locations such as ceremony and reception venues. You may also have to travel to vendors to pick things up.

Any time you are away from the office, you risk missing a call from someone who wants to hire you. A cell phone enables you to check messages on your voice mail and return calls as soon as possible. You should be able to get a cell phone from the company that provides your business line — or even pick one up at your local shopping mall.

Of course, you would not take a call when you are with a client for the same reason it's not a good idea to have call waiting on your business line — you want the person you are speaking with to feel that they are important to you, which will not happen if you interrupt your conversation to speak with someone else. So keep your cell phone on vibrate mode instead of ring.

5.2.3 Equipment and Supplies

In addition to telephones, you will need a variety of office equipment and supplies for your business. The initial cost of these items can come as a bit of a surprise to new business owners. However, once your office is stocked up, your ongoing expenses should be minimal.

Check with your local office supply stores, such as Staples and Office Depot, to find out about sales. The sales reps who work there can also be of assistance when it comes to getting help putting together everything you need for your office.

Computer

If you don't already have a computer, you should consider buying or leasing one for your business as soon as you can afford it. In addition to a computer and printer, it's a good idea to get the following:

- Zip drive or CD-RW (rewriteable CD drive) so you can back up your files

- Scanner or digital camera so you can e-mail photos of weddings you have planned and upload them to your website

- Surge protector to protect your computer from power surges

Software

Many computers already have the basic software needed to run a business. While Microsoft Office and other programs that came with your computer can be used in your business, the following types of programs can make your work easier. You can find them online or buy them from your local office supply store. Note that although these programs can be helpful to your business, they are not essential.

Bookkeeping

A bookkeeping program such as QuickBooks or Quicken can help you keep track of your income and expenses most efficiently.

Database

To keep track of your customers, including up to date contact information, you can use a database program that came with your computer (if you have MS Office, you could use MS Outlook) or you could buy a database program such as ACT! or Filemaker Pro.

Wedding Planning Software

This software can help keep track of every aspect of the wedding, including: guest lists, vendors, budgets, to-do lists, and details of the ceremony, reception, and even the honeymoon. Prices of the programs mentioned below range from free to $289.

There are numerous wedding industry websites that offer free online tracking of wedding details. For example, **www.ezwedding planner.com** has an excellent free online program. The biggest benefit to signing up with this service is that you will be sent periodic e-mail reminders each time a certain wedding task needs to be co-ordinated (although you will also be sent advertising e-mails from time to time). To sign up, you will need to provide your name, address, e-mail, and the wedding date and the names of the bride and groom.

If you decide to buy wedding planning software, make sure it can be used to keep track of multiple weddings. (Some companies will let you use a free trial version so you can decide if it's right for you.) Check out My Wedding Organizer at **www.weddingsoft.com** and Wedding Magic Pro at **www.frogwaresoftware.com** and look for others by doing a search for "wedding planning software."

There are also a number of professional event planner software packages available. Although quite costly, you may find one of these programs helpful to your business. Meeting Planner Plus has been a leader in the planning software market for years. It costs $1,995, and is available at **http://certain.com/Products** or by calling 888-237-8246.

Other Equipment and Supplies

Fax Machine and Photocopier

Both of these are optional. You may be able to use fax software that you have on your computer or go to the local copy shop when you need photocopies. If you think it will be more convenient to have them in your office, consider getting a combination fax/printer/scanner/copier unit.

Calculator

A good desktop calculator or adding machine can make your job much easier. Wedding planners are constantly working with budgets and other numbers so a machine with a tape readout is helpful.

Electronic Organizer

PDAs (personal digital assistants) like the Palm Pilot are essentially digital day-planners. A large assortment of affordable PDAs are on the market and you might consider managing your calendar using this technology. They allow you to synchronize with the calendar on your desktop computer, and allow you to access the Internet and your e-mail utilities.

Alternately, a small wireless device called the BlackBerry allows you to send and receive e-mail (using your thumbs to type) while on the go. You can surf the web, make phone calls, or even set up conference calls. The BlackBerry software includes a calendar, task list, address book, other features that may be useful for a wedding planner on the go.

File Cabinet

You'll need to organize and store information you receive from vendors, as well as keep files for each client. Your desk may have drawers that can hold files, but you will probably eventually need a file cabinet. Your options include two-door or four-door filing cabinets, or you may find a lateral file cabinet with a wood finish that fits beautifully with the rest of your office furniture.

Supplies

Of course you will need the supplies any business needs, including pens and pencils, paper, stapler, clips, Post-Its, scissors, tape, corrective tape or fluid, etc.

Stationery

Your stationery should present a consistent image, and promote you as a successful professional. You will need:

- Business cards

- Business stationery (letterhead and envelopes)

- A brochure describing your business and your services (see the section on marketing your business for ideas)

Beautiful stationery can help reassure prospective clients that you have a good eye and can make their weddings look beautiful too. Consider using heavy textured papers, raised printing, and a professional design. Check around for prices at print shops or office supply stores.

If your start-up finances are limited, you might want to consider getting free business cards from VistaPrint.com. They offer color business cards on heavy paper stock, available in a number of different designs. In return for the free cards (all you pay is shipping, which starts at around $7) they print their logo and "Business Cards are free at VistaPrint.com" on the back of the card near the bottom so you still have room to write something on the back if you want to. If you don't want anything printed on the back, you can get 250 cards for only $29.99 plus shipping. Visit **www.VistaPrint.com** or phone (800) 721-6214.

5.2.4 Insurance

Once you have equipped your office, you should protect what you have. However, insurance is one thing many small business owners would rather not worry about. It may seem like something that costs you time and money, but doesn't contribute to your business. But in fact, having insurance could save your business one day.

Types of Insurance

Property Insurance

Property insurance protects the contents of your business (e.g. your computer, any supplies, etc.) in case of fire, theft, or other losses. If you have a home office, your business property may not be covered by your homeowner's policy.

Errors and Omissions

This type of insurance protects you in case you make a mistake or have a misunderstanding with a client (for example, if something important wasn't done because you thought the bride was going to take care of it).

Insurance for You

If your family depends on your income, you may want to consider life insurance or disability insurance. Other types of personal insurance include health insurance or dental insurance (if you're not covered under a spouse's plan).

More Information

There are other types of insurance, and many different levels of coverage available for each type. An insurance broker (check the Yellow Pages) can advise you of your options and shop around for the best rates for you. Or you may be able to get insurance through a professional association for wedding planners (see section 5.5).

5.2.5 Employees and Contractors

You may be working on your own when you first start your business, but at some point you could decide to hire people to work with you. For example, you might hire an assistant, other wedding planners, or someone to help market your company.

Whenever you hire someone, you will either sign them on as employees or as contractors. What's the difference?

- Employees are trained by you. Contractors were trained elsewhere.

- Employees work only for you. Contractors may have their own customers and work for other event planning firms.

- Employees are paid on a regular basis. Contractors are paid per project.

- Employees work for a certain amount of hours. Contracted workers set their own hours, as long as they get the job done.

- Employees can be fired or quit. Contractors can't be fired in the usual way while they are working under contract. You may decide to have them stop working on a project, but you will be obliged to pay them according to your contractual agreement unless you are able to renegotiate the contract or successfully sue them if you are unhappy with their work. (Of course, that would only be in extreme cases; it is best to avoid lawsuits altogether!)

As a wedding planner, if you hire individuals to provide services such as music or photography, they will likely be self-employed contractors (who you will find through word of mouth or even the Yellow Pages). However, the other people who work for your company may be either employees or contractors, and there are different tax requirements for both. For more information about employment taxes, contact the IRS. You can find information at **www.irs.gov** by clicking on "Businesses."

Before you hire, check with your local department of labor to find out all the rules and regulations required as an employer. Other state and federal rules and regulations that may apply to you include health and safety regulations, Workers' Compensation, and unemployment insurance. Check the resources provided at the start of this chapter for excellent advice on hiring employees and contractors.

5.2.6 Finances

Start-Up Funding

Depending on how you set up your business, the cost of starting your wedding planning firm might range from almost nothing to thousands of dollars. Obviously, your start-up expenses will be much higher if you decide to rent space and buy equipment (e.g. to make wedding cakes).

You will also need to consider your "working capital" requirements. This is the money you will need for the day-to-day operation of your wedding planning company. If you are buying supplies for the wedding you can ask for a deposit (see the section on "setting your fees"). But there are other expenses that will come out of your pocket before you get your first client — such as business cards, telephone, etc.

Many entrepreneurs are optimistic about how much money they will earn from their business, and how quickly they will earn it. While you may be tremendously successful right from the start and exceed your own expectations, it is wise to be prepared for the possiblity it may take longer than expected until your business is earning enough to support you.

A standard rule of thumb is to have six months living expenses set aside beyond your start-up costs. Or you might consider remaining at your current job and working part-time on your wedding planning business until it is established.

Depending on the start-up costs you calculate in your business plan, you may find you have all the money you need to get started in your savings account (or available to spend on your credit cards). If your own resources won't cover all the things you would like to do with your wedding planning firm, you will need to look for financing.

One place to look for financing is from family members. They may be willing to invest in your company or give you a loan to help you get started. To avoid any misunderstandings, it's wise to get any agreements in writing even with family members.

If you decide to approach a bank for a business loan, be prepared. Write a loan proposal that includes detailed information about your business, how much money you want to borrow, what you plan to do with the money, and so on. Some good advice about financing can be found at the SBA and Nolo sites given at the start of this chapter.

Also look into the Small Business Administration business assistance programs. The SBA has a Loan Guarantee Program that provides loans to small businesses. Contact your local SBA office or check out **www.sba.gov/financing**.

Keeping Track of Your Money

There are a variety of resources available to help you keep track of your business income and expenses.

Financial Institution

The first of these resources is a financial institution – bank, trust company, or credit union – where you will open your business checking account. You can shop around to find a financial institution that is supportive of small business, or use the same one that you use for your personal banking. In addition to your checking account, a financial institution may provide you with:

- A corporate credit card you can use to make purchases for your business

- A merchant credit card account if you are planning to retail products such as wedding cakes or decorations (this enables you to accept credit card payments from your customers)

- A line of credit in case you want to pay up front for some supplies before you get paid by a customer

Bookkeeping System

Your bookkeeping system is a record of your expenses and income. To keep track of your expenses, you will need to keep copies of all receipts. This can sometimes be a challenge for new business owners who might have a habit of tossing out receipts for small items (or not asking for receipts in the first place). However, you are likely to have numerous small expenses related to your business, and these can add up.

The cup of coffee you buy for a prospective customer, the latest issue of a wedding magazine, the mileage you travel to a client's house, the pack of paper you pick up at the office supply store, the admission charge for a bridal fair — these and many other expenses should be accounted for so you can minimize your taxes. And, of course, knowing exactly where your money is going will help you plan better and cut back on any unnecessary expenses. So make it a habit to ask for a receipt for every expense related to business.

If you have the time, you can do your own bookkeeping. As mentioned in the section on software, there are programs available, such as Quicken or QuickBooks, which can make the job much easier for you. The **Quicken.com** website offers some good advice to help you with managing your finances and developing your business.

If you find yourself so busy with wedding planning work that you don't have time to do your own bookkeeping, consider hiring a part-time bookkeeper on a contract basis to do your bookkeeping for you. Depending on how busy you are, it may take the bookkeeper a few hours per week to get your books up to date and balance them with your bank statements. You can find a bookkeeper through word of mouth or checking the Yellow Pages.

Financial Experts

Just as people will hire an expert (you!) to plan their wedding, you may want to hire experts to assist with your finances. An accountant or tax advisor can be expensive (e.g. you might pay $100 per hour compared to the $20 per hour you might pay a bookkeeper). However, their advice could possibly save you hundreds or even thousands of dollars at tax time. If you're not able to find an accountant or tax advisor through word of mouth, you can try the Yellow Pages.

Of course, the way to earn a lot of money is by getting people to hire you.

5.3 Marketing Your Business

Your wedding was absolutely beautiful and your reception was fabulous! How did you do it? I'm trying to get ready for my own wedding, and I can't believe all the things that have to be handled.

My wedding planner is (your name). I'm delighted with the job she did. Would you like her telephone number?

This is an example of the way many wedding planners find clients — through word of mouth. As you probably know from personal experience, a recommendation from a friend is perhaps the most powerful form of advertising that exists.

But don't despair if you are just starting out. In this section of the guide you will find a variety of ideas to help you attract clients. And once you have done a great job for those first few clients, you can start attracting more through word of mouth.

5.3.1 Your Portfolio and Promotional Tools

A promotional tool is something you give or show to a prospective customer in order to promote your service. In addition to your business card, your promotional tools might include a portfolio, website, and brochures.

Your Portfolio

A portfolio shows examples of your work and may include the following:

- Photographs of weddings

- Testimonial letters from couples you have planned weddings for

- Anything else that shows your skill as a wedding planner

A portfolio offers a prospective customer proof that you have the skills to do the job. Read on to find out how to get items for your portfolio, and how to put it together.

Photographs

They say a picture is worth a thousand words and nowhere is this truer than when you are trying to sell yourself as being creative, imaginative and organized.

As mentioned in chapter 3, try to arrange to get photographs from every wedding you work on. In fact, with the first few weddings you plan for friends or relatives you might offer your wedding planning services for free in exchange for photographs to put into your portfolio. While you won't include every photograph in your portfolio, it is a good idea to have as many photos as possible to choose from.

Even if this is the first wedding you have planned, you can pull together a portfolio. In lieu of photographs of previously planned weddings you can use pictures from brochures and magazines to paint a picture of the various types of weddings you will help organize. Take a look at wedding planner sites. By and large you will notice pictures of the bride and groom, decorated tables from the reception, pictures of unusual ceremony settings and accoutrements like cakes, limos, etc. Ask vendors (photographers, venues, cake decorators, invitation engravers etc.) for permission to use their brochures in your portfolio to give couples an idea of what is possible and trendy.

If you have a camera and can take decent photos, you can create your own photographs. For example, you could decorate your own dining room table or construct a balloon archway. As soon as you've planned a wedding or two you will have pictures from an actual event and can drop the other items from your portfolio.

In addition to the traditional wedding photographs of the ceremony and bridal party, you should get photos of specific details including the flowers, decorations, wedding cake, table settings, and anything else that illustrates your work.

As mentioned, one way to get some ideas for types of photos to include in your own portfolio is by looking at online portfolios of other professional wedding planners. Check out portfolios at bridal shows, or do an online search for "wedding planner" and "portfolio."

When selecting photographs, remember that your portfolio should be a collection of your best work. Most couples do not have time to look through hundreds of photographs, so be selective about what to include. One suggested guideline is to choose 8-10 photographs per wedding (if you have that many different photos). It's ideal if you have planned several different types of weddings so you can show some variety in your work. If not, simply use what you have.

Once you have selected your photos, you can arrange them in a photo album or put them into a portfolio case or binder (see the section below on assembling your portfolio).

Letters of Recommendation

The best letters of recommendation are those written by couples you have done wedding planning work for. However, you can also include letters of recommendation from past employers, assuming the letters say good things about your abilities in areas that are important in the wedding planning business, such as interpersonal skills and organizational ability. You can also include appropriate thank-you notes you have received.

As was emphasized in chapter 3, every time you plan a wedding for someone – even a friend or family member (preferably with a different last name from yours!) – ask for a letter of recommendation.

When you ask for a letter, keep in mind that many people are busy so they are more likely to do what you ask if you can make it as easy as possible. To help get the kind of recommendation letter you want, and make the job easier on the person writing the letter, you could supply a list of points they might mention. For example:

- What you did (write it out for them — chances are you remember exactly what you did more clearly than they might)

- You saved them money by finding the best vendors

- You got along well with everyone you worked with

- You came up with many creative ideas

- You listened and delivered exactly what they wanted

- You handled every detail so they didn't have to worry about a thing

- Everyone has commented on how beautiful the wedding was

Of course all these things don't have to be included in a single letter! The specifics will depend on the particular job you did, but even a few glowing sentences can help you look good to customers.

If you feel your relative or friend will not write a great letter, even with some specific suggestions of what to include, you can offer to compose the letter yourself and have them simply supply the signature. You should have a couple of different letters written specifically for this purpose and propose one of them as an alternative.

Sample Reference Letter

Dear Wendy Wedding Planner,

Josh and I would like to take this opportunity to thank you again for the wonderful job you did on planning our big day! It was perfect and exactly what we had always hoped it would be.

Your ideas and creative little touches made our wedding day unique and one we will not soon forget.

You promised total organization and that is exactly what you delivered. What you didn't tell us was what a pleasure it would be to work with you. Your calming demeanor helped extinguish all the little fires that cropped up and for that we are thankful.

We will certainly recommend your service to family and friends and wish you success in the years to come.

Sincerely,
Britney Bride

P.S. The resort you suggested for our honeymoon was amazing. We are still glowing from the unforgettable experience.

TIP: A recommendation letter should preferably not mention that you worked for free. You want to give the impression that your work has value, and a customer may assume the reason you received such a glowing recommendation is because you didn't charge anything. Remember, good work is good work no matter how much you were paid for it.

What Else to Include

Your portfolio can include anything else that could impress someone who is considering hiring you. For example, if you have a certificate of membership in a wedding planning association or for completion of a wedding planning course, put the actual certificate in your portfolio. If that's not possible, include a photocopy or photograph of the certificate.

If your wedding planning business has been mentioned in a newspaper or magazine story, you could include a clipping or photocopy of the published article. Later in this chapter you will find information about how to write articles for publication, and other ways to establish your reputation as a wedding expert. Some wedding planners also include sample wedding timelines or other planning materials in their portfolios.

Putting It All Together

One possibility for displaying your portfolio items is to put everything into a professional looking three-ring binder with plastic sheet covers to protect the pages. If you wish, you can mount your photographs and other portfolio materials onto thin cardboard. All of these supplies are available from any office supply store.

Another possibility is to use a portfolio case, which you can buy at an art supply store (check the Yellow Pages). Portfolio cases comes in a variety of sizes (e.g. 11" x 14", 14" x 17", 17" x 22") and cost from about $15 to over $150, depending on the size, material, and how fancy you want it to be. However, clients are interested in what is inside the case, so you don't need to spend a lot of money on the case itself (e.g. you could get vinyl instead of leather).

In addition to preparing a portfolio to take with you to meetings, it's also a good idea to create an online portfolio (also known as a web portfolio). This is a selection of photos posted on a personal webpage which people can access at any time.

Website

A website is an excellent marketing tool for a wedding planner. Although it probably won't generate much business itself (people are not likely to search for a wedding planner online), your website can complement your other marketing efforts. When someone who is looking for a wedding planner sees your web address on your business card, in a Yellow Pages ad, or elsewhere, they can visit your website 24 hours a day to learn more about your services.

What to Include

Most wedding planners use their websites as a place to show examples of their work. As mentioned above, you can create an "online portfolio." This is a selection of photographs from different weddings that you have worked on.

On a page titled "Portfolio" you could publish "thumbnail" photos (small photos that can be clicked on to see a larger copy of the same photo). Or you could have a page with links to each wedding (listed by couples' names or by the type of wedding) that when clicked on go to a page for that wedding.

TIP: Before publishing any photos at your website, make sure you have written permission from the couple and photographer.

To explain what is in the photos, you could include captions, or a summary of wedding details, such as the ceremony location, flowers, reception menu, décor, etc. For example, for the music you could list the pieces performed during the ceremony, the first dance, etc., and describe the performers (e.g. "reception music performed by five piece jazz ensemble").

In addition to a portfolio, your website can include information such as:

- An "About Us" page which describes your experience planning weddings and includes a photograph of you

- An overview of the services you provide (e.g. planning the entire wedding, wedding day co-ordination, destination weddings, hourly consultations)

- Contact information (your company name, telephone number, e-mail address, and possibly other contact information such as a cell phone or pager number) could be included at the bottom of each page

- Testimonials from brides or couples that you have planned weddings for

- Your fees are optional (some wedding planners include them, while others prefer to discuss them in person with the couple); however you should mention if you offer a free consultation

- Any additional information that you think will help sell your services (e.g. benefits of hiring a wedding planner, wedding planning tips you have written)

You can get some ideas for your own website by seeing what other wedding planners have done with theirs. Visit some of the sites mentioned throughout this guide or check local Yellow Pages ads to find websites of wedding planners in your community.

Developing a Website

If you are already experienced at creating webpages, or learn quickly, you can design your website yourself using a program such as Microsoft's Front Page or Netscape Composer (free with the Netscape Browser).

Otherwise, it's a good idea to hire a professional web designer through word of mouth or the Yellow Pages. Of course, you should visit sample sites they have created before hiring them.

You may be able to put up free webpages through your Internet Service Provider (the company that gives you access to the Internet). To present a professional image, and make your web address easier for clients to remember, consider getting your own domain name such as www.yourcompany.com. There are a number of sites where you can search for and register a domain name. The most popular is Network Solutions at **www.netsol.com**.

Once you register your domain you will need to find a place to "host" it. Network Solutions provides that service, and your Internet Service Provider may also. You can find a wide variety of other companies that provide hosting services by doing an online search. (Do not use a free web hosting service unless you don't mind having your customers see pop-up ads for products like spy cameras!)

To help promote your site, do a search at Google.com for "wedding directory" to find numerous places you can list your site for free. You should promote your site whenever possible, such as listing your website in your other marketing materials.

Brochures

You can give brochures to prospective clients you meet at networking events and bridal shows, or who phone after seeing an ad and ask to have information mailed to them. Your brochure should have your company name and contact information (including your web address). It can also include some of the information you have on your website, such as:

- One or more wedding photographs

- Benefits of hiring a wedding planner

- Services you offer

- A photograph of you

- Some testimonials

Your brochure can be folded in three, with printing on both sides of the sheet, or you can simply print a one page flyer which could also be pinned up on bulletin boards.

If you are printing only a few copies of your brochure, you may be able to find nice paper at your local office supply store which you can run through the printer connected to your home computer. If you aren't able to produce brochures on your home computer, or if you need hundreds of brochures (for example, if you are participating in a bridal show), it may be faster and cheaper for you to have your brochures professionally printed. Check the Yellow Pages under "Printers," or use the printing services of your local office supply store, such as Staples.

Once you have your brochures and other promotional tools, you will be able to give them to people you meet through networking.

5.3.2 Networking

Networking, or "schmoozing," as it's been called, can be a little intimidating at first but is a valuable marketing tool and one that gets easier every time you use it. So what exactly is networking? Simply put, it is interacting informally with people for the purpose of finding new clients. The people you network with can either be prospective clients, or anyone who could refer you to clients.

As previously mentioned, an example of a good networking opportunity is attending a bridal fair. You have the opportunity to meet with possible future clients (brides-to-be and their friends) as well as vendors who might refer you to clients. You can meet even more brides by having your own booth at a bridal fair (see section 5.3.5). Here are some other ways to network.

Sample Letter to Family

Dear Aunt Mary,

I hope this letter finds you well. Mom tells me you are planning a trip to Paris. I hope you have a wonderful time, and I'm very happy to hear you will be back in time for next summer's family reunion.

I am writing to you with some exciting news. You will probably recall how as a child I always loved planning weddings for my Barbie and Ken dolls and how I drove my mother crazy asking for scraps of fabric to fashion into wedding dresses. Well, I've decided to take my passion for everything wedding-related and turn it into a business.

Recently I took related online courses and am now a certified wedding planner. Starting your own business is certainly scary and it took a big leap of faith to leave my full-time job for a part-time one, but I'm sure it will be worth it.

I've been told that one of the best ways to find new clients is through word of mouth and I'm hoping you will pass my business card to anyone in your church group who has a newly engaged daughter or son or knows of someone who is thinking of getting married.

I hope you enjoy Paris and look forward to seeing you very soon.

Love,
Wendy

Family and Friends

Wedding planners can follow the tried and tested method used by real estate agents, who are networking experts. Family and friends are usually targeted first with the hope they will be kind enough to pass on your business card or name at a suitable opportunity.

Compose a letter (you can keep it fairly informal if you like) telling your family and friends that you have opened a business as a wedding planner. Tell them your qualifications and what types of services you provide. Include a few business cards in the envelope and encourage the recipient to pass them on to everyone they know who may be planning a wedding in the future. A sample letter is on the facing page.

You can also send a more generic version of a letter to family and friends by simply omitting personal items.

Vendors

Earlier in this guide you were given advice on developing relationships with vendors with the aim of learning about wedding planning and finding resources to recommend to your clients.

Another very important reason to develop relationships with vendors is so they can refer business to you. Arrange meetings with as many vendors as possible — bridal shops, reception venues, florists, photographers, limousine companies, etc. Remember, you are not only there to get to know what products and services each vendor supplies but to give them the chance to get to know you.

Bring business cards and brochures and prepare to sell yourself and your bridal services. Tell the person you are speaking with that you believe in mutually rewarding relationships and would be pleased to bring or send your clients to them and that in turn, you would appreciate it if they would pass on your name to their prospective clients that have not contracted a wedding planner.

As was mentioned earlier, it is important for you to foster a good working relationship with many vendors. It is true that people do business with those they like and respect, and if they like and respect you they will recommend you. Following the tips in the sections on working with vendors and building relationships can help you build a great network.

Networking Clubs

Another valuable form of networking is through a networking club. Networking clubs usually have a formal structure in place. Each club will have a target group of clients and include one member from different industries (e.g. insurance, financial planning, law, professional photography, real estate, etc.) to reach those in the target group. Each member of the club is expected to bring a certain number of leads to the group each week or month.

Fees will vary but can be as low as the cost of breakfast once a week, and you may also be required to take a turn serving on the executive board. In addition to the marketing opportunity, benefits of joining may include discounts on services provided by other members of the group. To become a member you are either recommended to the group by an existing member, or you might approach the group and ask to sit in as an observer for a meeting or two, and from there get accepted.

The quality of the participants will differ with every group and it is important to keep this in mind when searching for one to join. Most will allow a trial period before you commit to them and they commit to you. You may be asked to give a short presentation on exactly what you do and what quality you can bring to the group.

You should do some checking around first before deciding which one to join. For example, a group that includes a lawyer, insurance agent, realtor, travel agent and photographer would find value in networking with someone who has leads to newly married couples. A group that included a computer reseller, book publisher, retirement planner and Internet service provider would not be a great mix. Don't forget, you want the other professionals in the club to provide solid leads for you as well.

One way to find a networking club is through word of mouth. Ask individuals in a sales oriented job, such as insurance agents, financial planners, computer sales, car sales, travel agents. You may also be able to find networking groups online. Business Network International has more than 3,400 chapters in cities around the world. Visit **www.bni.com** or phone 1-800-688-9394.

Other Organizations

Another excellent way to network is by joining associations that prospective clients and vendors may belong to. Some examples include:

- Service clubs (such as Rotary Club or Kiwanis Club)

- Business organizations (such as your local chamber of commerce)

- Clubs that attract the wealthy (e.g. golf, yachting, country clubs)

Other organizations you could get involved with include cultural organizations and churches. You will probably find scores of organizations in your community that you could get involved with. So get involved with those that interest you, as well as those that could lead to business.

Membership fees may vary from $20 to hundreds or thousands of dollars (the latter if you want to join an exclusive country club or private golf club). Fortunately, many non-exclusive organizations will let you attend one or two events for a nominal fee so you can decide if you want to join.

You can find organizations through word of mouth, in your local telephone directory, or online. Here are a couple to get you started:

Executive Women International
Phone: (801) 355-2800
Fax: (801) 355-2852
E-mail: ewi@executivewomen.org
Website: **www.executivewomen.org**

World Chamber of Commerce Directory
Phone: (970) 663-3231
Fax: (970) 663-6187
Website: **www.chamberofcommerce.com**

While membership in any organization can potentially be valuable, simply attending "networking" functions is not the only way to make an impact on prospective clients. To make the most out of your membership in an association, there are several things you can do to raise your profile, including:

- Serve on a committee

- Write articles for the association newsletter

- Do volunteer work such as offering to decorate for events

- Run for election to the Executive Committee

The more involved you are in an association, the more likely you are to connect with prospective clients or people who can refer you to clients.

5.3.3 Advertising

While networking can be a particularly effective way to get business for your wedding planning company, you may also be able to attract some clients through advertising.

Yellow Pages

You have probably used the Yellow Pages many times. But before you buy an ad for your own business, you should carefully investigate the costs compared to the potential return. Many new business owners find a Yellow Pages ad does not make the phone ring off the hook with buyers. If someone does respond to your ad, they may be "shopping around," so you must be prepared to invest time as well as advertising dollars if you use this method of advertising.

To minimize your risk, you might want to consider starting with a small display ad, such as a 1/8 page ad. If you can get your hands on a previous year's edition of your local Yellow Pages, compare the ads for wedding planners from year to year. If you notice others have increased or decreased the size of their ads, this can give you an indication of what might work for you.

Also, if you are doing information interviews (as suggested in chapter 3) you can ask the wedding planners you speak with about how well their Yellow Pages ads are working for them.

You can either design the ad yourself, have the Yellow Pages design it for you, or hire a designer. Take a look at the ads in the weddings category of your current Yellow Pages for ideas. If you are interested in advertising, contact your local Yellow Pages to speak with a sales rep. Check the print version of your phone book for contact information.

Magazines

Magazine advertising can be expensive, and may not generate the results you want unless you do it repeatedly. (It has been estimated that many people need to see an advertisement three to seven times before they buy.)

In an article in *USA Today*, Steve Strauss, a lawyer, author and business expert, says there are five reasons why good ads sometimes fail, including running the ad in the wrong media and/or on the wrong day, making your offer too weak to attract customers and not advertising with enough frequency to build awareness of your product.

If you choose to buy advertising, it will probably be most cost-effective to place ads in small local magazines or newspapers. The publications you advertise in will usually design your ad for an additional cost, and give you a copy of the ad to run in other publications.

At least once a year, many newspapers publish special sections that focus on weddings. Contact the publication's advertising department to find out when their next wedding section will be published. However, you will get much better results if you can get free publicity instead of paying for advertising.

5.3.4 Free Media Publicity

The traditional media are magazines, newspapers, radio and television, and the term "online media" has come to describe Internet publications. When a business gets publicity in a magazine article, newspaper story, radio or television talk show, or well-known website, it can result in a tremendous amount of new business. Here are some ways wedding planners can get publicity.

Press Releases

A press release is a brief document that you submit to the media with the aim of getting publicity for your business. The ideal press release is a single page (less than 500 words) and is written like a news story. If you write something that sounds like an advertisement, it is unlikely to be published. You can find numerous online resources to help you write a press release, including **www.publicityinsider.com/release.asp**.

Most magazines and newspapers publish contact information for their editors. Newspapers may have dozens of editors, so make sure you send your submission to the appropriate one (for example, the Lifestyle Editor). As an alternative to writing a press release, you could find out who the editor is, and either phone or send a brief "pitch letter" by e-mail, fax or mail to suggest an idea for a story.

In your pitch, remember to focus on something that will be interesting to readers. For example, you might suggest a story on how to save money on weddings, wedding etiquette for dealing with difficult situations, or unique locations to hold wedding ceremonies. Do some brainstorming or consider a story based on the most common kinds of questions customers ask you.

While it is not necessary to submit photographs to a daily newspaper editor (most newspapers have their own photographers), photographs may help attract the editor's attention. They might also be published in a smaller magazine, newspaper or newsletter that doesn't have a photographer on staff.

If you send photos (remember to make sure you have permission from the people in the photos as well as the photographer), put them in an attractive two-pocket folder with your business card and a cover letter. Then follow up a week later with a phone call.

Write an Article or Column

One of the best ways to establish yourself as an expert is to write articles or a column for a newspaper, magazine, newsletter, or website. While it can be tough to break into large daily newspapers, there may be an opportunity to write for smaller newspapers, local magazines, and online publishers.

You could write on any topic related to planning a wedding, or propose an "Ask the Wedding Planner" column where you would answer questions from readers. The length and frequency of your column will depend on the publication. You might produce a weekly 500-word column for a local newspaper or website that is updated frequently, or a monthly 1,000-word column for a newsletter or magazine.

Make sure your article or column provides valuable information to the publication's readers. As with press releases, articles that sound like an ad for your services are not likely to get published.

Once you have written your first column or article, phone or e-mail the editor to ask if they would be interested in seeing it. If so, they will probably ask you to e-mail it. If they want to publish it, they may offer to pay you. However, even if they don't pay, you should consider letting them publish it in return for including a brief bio and your contact information at the end of the article or column.

Television and Radio Talk Shows

Phone local radio and TV shows to let them know you are available to provide wedding planning advice to their viewers or listeners. Shows that might be appropriate include morning shows and afternoon talk shows. The person to contact is the producer of each show.

The producer may ask you to send them some information, so be prepared to e-mail or fax a few paragraphs about yourself, along with a list of frequently asked questions. (These are questions their audience would likely be interested in knowing the answer to. You can put any questions you like on the list, but chances are whatever you find people asking your advice about are questions that an audience would be interested in as well.) TV is a visual medium, so it's also a good idea to suggest some things they could shoot you doing, in their studio or elsewhere.

5.3.5 Bridal Shows

If you live in a medium to large city, you've probably attended a trade show at some point. There are many types of trade shows geared to special interest groups like home improvement, outdoor sports, arts and crafts and everything in between. Wedding tradeshows – usually called "bridal shows" or "bridal fairs" – are held in most major cities in North America and draw huge crowds of future brides and grooms and their friends and family. Exhibitors include wedding planners, bakers, travel agents, florists, bridal fashion retailers, limousine rentals, and others.

These shows are usually two to three days in duration and can attract up to 10,000 visitors per day. Exhibitors may have either a draped table with a simple backdrop, or a full-scale booth with side and back walls and racks for displaying merchandise. Your booth could be as simple as a banquet-sized table to hold your promotional materials.

Table and Booth Fees

Most shows charge hundreds of dollars for a booth. The exact cost will vary depending on the particular show, the location, the number of people expected to attend, and the amount of space you require. To give only a couple of examples, we found booth fees ranging from $80 for a bridal show in El Dorado County, California, to $700 for the 2005 Bridal Extravaganza in Charlotte, North Carolina.

To save money, you could partner with another non-competing exhibitor and share a booth space. An example of a good match would be a venue. The benefit in this pairing would be that most couples will rent a space to hold their reception or ceremony (except those that hold backyard ceremonies) but not all of them will have thought of using the services of a wedding planner. Similarly, a couple may be interested in hiring a wedding planner but have not yet decided on a venue.

You and the other exhibitor could each suggest the services of the other to the couple. You could agree to say something like "Have you hired your wedding planner yet?" or "Have you decided where to hold your reception yet?"

Where to Find Bridal Shows

There are a number of good websites to help you find local bridal shows, including Bridal Show Producers International at **www.bspishows.com** and Wedding Details list of bridal shows at **www.weddingdetails.com/shows**. However, not every state or province is listed at these sites. If your location is not listed, call your local convention center or chamber of commerce for information. You can also search online using your city name and "bridal show," "bridal fair," or "wedding show" as keywords.

To book space as an exhibitor you will need to know how much space you require and what your needs will be. You will likely be required to sign a contract and pay a certain percentage of the cost up front. Each show will be handled differently and the show's producers should be able to tell you exactly what you need to do to book space. Many bridal shows now have their own websites and provide registration information as well as site maps and logistical information.

Setting up Your Booth

You should bring business cards (make sure the information is current and that you have a large number of them), your company brochures and portfolio for display at your booth.

If you provide a service that is out of the ordinary for most planners, you should prominently display these items. For instance, you may special-ize in small token silk arrangements for the bride to use for the bouquet toss or you might be an excellent seamstress and offer a free small satin monogrammed bag for the bride to carry. Bring samples of your best work and be ready to discuss prices and options.

When you speak with prospective clients, toss in a few of the ideas you have for creating a spectacular wedding (but don't give away too much for free). To arrange consultations and discuss possible bookings, bring an appointment book or calendar of events you already have on the books. This is very important to know if you are a one-person operation and have already been booked for full wedding day co-ordination on the specific day a potential client is interested in.

> **TIP:** If you don't have an assistant, find a partner or even a spouse or close friend to help out at the show. The days can be long and tiring, and you won't want to close down your booth to take breaks.

5.3.6 Creative Marketing Ideas

Put on Your Own Bridal Show

Running your own mini-show can be a great way to promote yourself — and you may even earn a profit from the show itself.

Before you start advertising or sending out invitations to the general public, canvass vendors in your neighborhood geared to the wedding industry to gauge the level of interest from them. A show without exhibitors wouldn't make much sense. Businesses to ask include services that pamper the bride (hair salons, massage therapists, day spas) plus the usual wedding vendors (caterers, florists, limousine services, photographers, reception venues, etc.), travel agents, and liquor/wine stores or representatives. Try to get each business to donate some sort of prize or prize package as a way of attracting a crowd.

If you can convince enough vendors that a small intimate show would be valuable to their business, strike a committee of interested parties and find a venue to hold the show. The venue could be a church, community center, banquet room of a local hotel, or school gymnasium.

If you keep costs low and charge the exhibitors a small fee you may be able to have the event free to the public and attract a larger crowd than if you charge people to attend. (There are people who will not attend trade shows that demand a paid admission, as they feel they are paying to shop, which one would normally do free of charge.) Alternatively, charge a small amount for admission and a small amount for booth space (or per table) to cover the cost of the venue and table rentals, advertising cost etc. When all is said and done, making a bit of money from admissions would be a bonus; however, the focus of this activity is to get your name out there and find new clients.

Debbe, a distributor of cosmetics and nutritional supplements, hosts an annual women's evening, showcasing services and products that are of interest to women. Many of the businesses that rent a table or booth space are small home-based businesses or those just entering the marketplace. She charges a nominal admittance fee to help defray the cost of the room rental and has convinced local businesses to give away samples of their products to entice people to attend. For example, a massage-chair is set up to provide a free shoulder rub, and samples of chocolates and other goodies are given away.

Offer a Bridal Shower or Bridesmaid's Lunch Service

Everyone is busy these days, and what better way to get to meet a lot of brides than to offer a "Shower Hosting Service"? You could offer to do as much or as little as you are comfortable with.

Start by hosting a shower for a close friend who is getting married and discreetly mention that you provide this service as part of your wedding planning business. For example, you could team up with a catering company or restaurant (or, if you're talented, you could do the cooking yourself) and offer a basic shower or luncheon package. It could include:

- Printing and mailing invitations

- Maintaining RSVP list

- Organizing gift suggestions or registry

- Catering and onsite management

Give a Speech

Another way to market your services to prospective clients and vendors is to offer to speak about wedding planning. Many associations have speakers for breakfast meetings, luncheons, workshops, and annual conventions.

Ask friends and acquaintances if they belong to any groups that have presentations from speakers. Organizations that might be interested in hearing you talk may include women's groups and vendors' associations. To prepare a talk that the audience will find interesting, consider what their needs are. For example, if you're speaking to a business net-working group, you might talk on "How to Promote Your Services to New Brides," while a women's group might be interested in hearing tips on how to plan a successful event.

If you give a good talk and offer useful advice, you will be seen as an expert. As long as there are people in the audience who need wedding planning services (or who can refer you to people who do), this can be an excellent way to attract clients.

While you probably will not be paid for your presentations, it can be an excellent opportunity to promote your business. Your company name may be published in the organization's newsletter, it will be mentioned by the person who introduces you, you can distribute business cards and brochures, and you will be able to mingle with attendees before and after your presentation. (You may get a free breakfast or lunch, too!)

5.4 Working with Clients

Congratulations! A couple is interested in hiring you to plan their wedding. Let's look at what happens now.

5.4.1 Setting Your Fees

Before meeting with your first paying clients, you will need to decide how much you are going to charge for your services. The question may come up before your first meeting, so you will need to be prepared with an answer.

Fees for planning or co-ordinating weddings are as varied as services offered by planners themselves. Some prefer to charge a flat rate for their services based on a percentage of the total wedding budget, while others offer individually priced packages according to the type and num-ber of services the client desires. To help you decide which fee arrangement(s) would be best for your business, here are typical ways wedding planners charge for their services:

- Consultation fee

- Percentage of the wedding budget

- No charge to client (wedding planner earns commissions from vendors)

- Hourly fee

- Flat fee

Consultation Fee

Many wedding planners give a one-half to one-hour free initial consultation. In such cases, this first meeting is simply an opportunity to learn more about what the clients need and explain how your services can benefit them.

However, other wedding planners start charging from the first meeting. As mentioned in chapter 2, instead of having you plan the entire wedding, some clients may want a consultation only. The purpose of this consultation meeting could be to assist the bride and groom with choosing vendors, set a planning calendar, give advice on etiquette issues, help with budget forecasting, etc.

Since you will actually be working, you should of course be paid for your services. You could charge your hourly fee (see below), based on a minimum number of hours.

Robbi Ernst III, founder of June Wedding Inc., and author of Great Wedding Tips from the Experts, says that a flat fee for a three-hour initial consultation may range from $175 in rural areas to as much as $500 in large cities.

As a beginning wedding consultant, you may choose to charge less than what experienced wedding planners charge. For example, even if you live in a large city you might offer a three-hour consultation for $150 to $200.

Percentage of Wedding Budget

Charging a percentage of the total wedding budget is a common way for wedding planners to charge for their services. A fee of 10-15% is the norm, although some wedding planners charge up to 20% of the budget.

This fee arrangement can work well when the guest list is fairly large. You will not want to offer this pricing if the event has a relatively small budget. For instance, a $5,000 total budget will only net the planner $500 at 10%, and even if you charge as much as 20% the fee will be only $1,000. If the client were to choose full-service wedding planning you could be doing an incredible amount of work for very little money.

If you do decide to price your services this way, determining the budget will be an important first step to ensure you can provide the service for that amount of money. For a typical traditional wedding of $22,000, a 15% fee would total $3,300.

Be aware that your clients may expect that if you are charging a percentage of the wedding budget, you will save them at least that amount on the wedding costs. **TodaysBride.com** says:

> "Keep in mind that hiring a wedding consultant will not be an added expense to the total budget. ... Remember, if the consultant charges, say, 15% of the total cost of the wedding, that means he or she must provide you with the wedding you want for 15% less than it would normally cost. In many cases, a good consultant can save you even more than that."

No Charge to Client

Some wedding planners offer their services free of charge to clients. They earn their money from commissions paid by vendors. The percentage commission will depend on how effective a negotiator you are. However, as mentioned earlier, many vendors will give you 10% off simply because you request a discount. (Discounts are normally passed along to the client.) If you have established a relationship with a vendor, they may offer you a higher percentage for referring business to them.

Receiving this type of "kickback" or "finder's fee" is viewed as unethical by many wedding planners, although it is standard practice in other industries. (For example, travel agents traditionally offered their services free of charge to travelers because they were paid a commission by airlines, hotels, and other travel vendors.)

When deciding whether to go this route with your business, consider that some clients (those who believe "you get what you pay for") may be skeptical of a wedding planner who charges no fee for their service. Also, clients who are shopping around may hear warnings from your competitors to beware of wedding planners who work for free because they take kickbacks.

One of the best reasons for a couple to hire a wedding planner is to reap the rewards and benefits of the planner's expertise in negotiating the lowest possible prices from vendors. If you are not passing the savings on to your client you run the risk of losing them to a planner that does. If you decide not to charge a fee, be prepared to address these objections by showing that the vendors you have chosen are reputable and reasonably priced.

Hourly Fee

If you are going to be providing partial wedding planning services, you might charge an hourly fee. Most wedding planners charge fees ranging from $25 to $150 per hour, although $50 per hour is typical.

You do not have to start at $25 per hour. In fact, you may want to charge a higher fee (such as $40 to $65 per hour) when you start because it may actually make some clients more likely to work with you. As mentioned, many believe "you get what you pay for" so they may assume a wedding planner who charges $50 per hour is more experienced or will do a better job than one who charges $25 per hour.

Flat Fee

Some clients may want to know up front what the total cost will be for your services. These clients prefer to pay a "flat fee" rather than an hourly fee so they know the cost will not go above a certain amount. There are several possible scenarios:

Flat Fee Based on Time Worked

In this case you might decide what your time is worth on an hourly, daily or weekly basis and charge according to the amount of time you feel each particular event will require. For example, if you are planning the rehearsal dinner, one shower and co-ordinating the day of the wedding and have determined it will take you 40 hours worth of time to organize and co-ordinate all of these, then simply multiply your applicable hourly fee by 40. If it takes you 50 hours you will not be compensated for the additional 10 hours you work. However, the more experience you acquire, the easier it will be to determine a flat fee for a particular job.

Flat Fee for Wedding Day Co-ordination

Often a bride and groom and their respective families have done all the legwork and the only thing missing is someone to make sure the wedding day itself is perfect (or as near to perfect as possible). Although the number of hours you spend may vary from one wedding to another, most wedding day co-ordinators charge a standard amount for this service, such as $1,500. Services provided could include co-ordinating either until the start of dinner or to the end of the evening.

Flat Fee for Specific Services

Another option is to charge a flat fee for a particular service, such as co-ordinating a vendor. The clients may want to take care of some of the details like shopping for flowers and tuxedos and choosing the venue, but do not want to be involved in securing the services of the DJ or caterer. In this case, you might charge a fee of $150 to $200 per vendor.

However, make sure you take all your costs into account. For example, if you have to make four trips to a vendor far across town (e.g. for meetings and to pick up and drop off materials), $150 would not be enough to compensate you for your time and travel expenses.

Other Fee Options

Once you have been planning weddings for a while, you may decide to revise your fees, or charge amounts based on different methods. For example, for wedding day co-ordination, some wedding planners charge both a flat fee and a percentage of vendor costs. Another option is to charge a fee based on the number of guests, with a set minimum. The downside to this is that the number of actual guests may be lower than the initial estimate. Make sure the minimum charged is enough, and do not hope to make more money by unexpected numbers of guests.

With more experience or education, you may also want to raise your fees. To give you an idea of what you can charge, here are some figures from Robbi Ernst III, founder of June Wedding Inc., and author of *Great Wedding Tips from the Experts*:

> "In rural areas, the preparation planning fee starts at $2,000; in metropolitan areas, the fee can start at $4,500. Add on another $1,500 in less-populated areas to $3,000 or more in larger cities, and you can have a full production wedding consultant who will be present to orchestrate and direct the rehearsal and wedding day. Obviously these fees can be much higher depending on the size and complexity of your wedding."

As you can see, you should give a lot of thought to setting your fees before you start your business, and be prepared for many scenarios. When deciding how much to charge, consider the services you provide, the size of your community, and what the local competition charges.

Another important factor to consider when designing your fee package is to determine what your overhead and administration costs are and ensure you are including a percentage of your costs into every event. For example, you may hire the services of an assistant for the actual wedding day and will have to consider charging extra for the additional person or add their fee directly into the overall budget or your package.

Getting Paid

Whatever type or combination of packages and service fees you decide is best for your company to offer, make sure you and your client agree to it in writing. Be as specific as possible about exactly what you will and, more importantly, will not provide for that stated fee. A sample contract appears in the next section, but you will need to revise it according to the specifics of your arrangement with your client.

For example, if they contract you for wedding day co-ordination services only, you could run into unnecessary conflict if you do not tell your client that you will not be overseeing the rehearsal. If your fee covers your service up to the dinner only, make sure you clearly indicate to the client that you will not be there to co-ordinate and troubleshoot during dinner, the cutting of the cake, throwing the bouquet and other events that happen during or after the dinner.

Alternatively, if the agreement is for you to co-ordinate the entire wedding day including the rehearsal, ceremony and reception you should also include the maximum number of hours you will work on the rehearsal day and wedding day (or a quit time), and list the hourly overtime charge for any hours worked over and above your stated maximum, and stipulate that a meal for the co-ordinator and any assistants should also be provided. It is always better to overstate what may seem obvious than to assume the client understands what is included.

One of the good things about being a wedding planner is that you do not have to wait until the wedding day to start getting paid. At the end of your initial consultation, if the clients want to go ahead, you can ask for a non-refundable deposit (e.g. $1,000 or more if you are offering full-service wedding planning) with the balance payable on the wedding day, or even a week before the wedding.

5.4.2 How to Do a Client Consultation

Telephone Interview

Unless you met your prospective clients at a bridal show or other live event, your first contact with a bride or couple will most likely be a short telephone interview.

For this reason, it is important that your telephone is always answered in a professional, friendly voice with your company name. Do not allow family members to answer your phone if you are not available, and be sure to have your voice mail pick up if you are running after a screaming child and the family dog. A harried response does not make a good first impression of someone who is supposed to be trained to stay calm, cool and collected during any crisis!

Most of your telephone interviews will be from couples searching for information on pricing and what a wedding planner does. Smart business people attempt to set up a face-to-face meeting to discuss their services more in-depth than what a phone call will allow, but you can use this first contact to set up the meeting. Sellers of time-share opportunities (those offers of free resort rooms you get in the mail) know that it is much easier to hang up the receiver than to walk away from a meeting. So how can you keep the person on the phone and convince them to meet with you? By gently taking control of the conversation and keeping your answers concise and focused on what a valuable service wedding planners provide to the bride – a stress-free wedding.

Your conversation could go something like this:

Bride: Hello. I'm looking for some information on how much you charge to do a wedding.

You: Thank you for calling. My name is: _____. May I get your name?

Bride: Betty Bride.

You: Would you prefer if I called you Betty or Ms. Bride?

Bride: Call me Betty.

You: Well, Betty, our company has many excellent packages available depending on the number of services the client prefers we handle. But we can also design a package especially for you. We are experts at negotiating and securing fair prices from our vendors and pass the savings on to you. Our services start at $150 and range from arranging vendors only to full-service planning including wedding day co-ordination. Have you had a chance to see our portfolio or any information on our company's services?

Bride: No. I just got your number from the phone book and thought I'd call. I'm not even sure I understand everything a wedding planner does.

You: Betty, I'm not sure what another wedding planner would tell you, but I can tell you my goal is to create a wedding as unique as you are while taking the worry, stress and time commitment off you, your fiancé and both families' shoulders. I offer a free one-hour initial consultation and I'd be pleased to meet with you to take the mystery out of what a wedding planner does. I have Tuesday, Thursday and Friday open — which day would be good for you?

There are many ways of delivering information on your packages to clients (e-mail, your website, brochures etc.) but the absolute best way to deliver your information is with a personal meeting.

If Betty Bride decides she'd rather get the information in the mail, send it at once. Make absolutely certain you spell her name correctly and repeat the address back to confirm it. Ask for her phone number for follow-up purposes, and mail your materials in an appropriately sized envelope (don't squish them in) and make sure you use the correct postage. Send a cover letter thanking her for her interest in your company and tell her you will follow up within a few days. Call in a few days to ensure she received the materials and ask if she has any questions.

If the couple says yes to a meeting, it is time for you to shine. Pull out all the stops and put all of your creative and marketing skills to the test.

Initial Consultation

The purpose of your initial consultation is to learn as much as possible about the bride and groom, and what they want, so you can show them how hiring you will help them achieve the wedding of their dreams.

Where Should the Meeting Take Place?

If you are fortunate enough to have an office outside your home and it is a nicely decorated space, by all means have the consultation in your office. You will be close to all of the materials you've gathered during your research and learning stage and will be able to answer questions with pictures as well as words.

Similarly, if you have a home office that is nicely decorated and free from interruptions (i.e. no children, barking dogs, etc.) and you are licensed to have a home-based business, have the meeting there.

If, on the other hand, you do not have either of these spaces available to you, you should meet at a spot you know will allow you to have a private and uninterrupted conversation. This could be the bride's home, her parents' home, or a private room in a tea-room or restaurant.

What You Should Bring to the Meeting

If the meeting takes place away from your home or office, be absolutely certain you come well prepared. Here are some items an organized wedding planner can bring to a client meeting:

- A list of questions to find out what the couple wants (see section 2.2.1)

- A notepad and pen to make notes

- Your portfolio

- References from past clients (friends or family included)

- Your business cards

- Your brochure, if you have one

- Price list and sample packages (e.g. full-service, wedding day only, etc.)

- Wedding planner checklists

- Brochures from preferred vendors

- A budget estimator (found in most wedding planner software programs) or one you've created yourself with spreadsheet software

- A calculator

- A two-year calendar or date book that includes the following year

- A blank contract

Although this initial consultation may be seen as only an opportunity for the client to assess whether they would like to hire a wedding planner or not, it is a good idea to come prepared to write up a contract (more on this later) and get the clients to outline their preferences.

What to Wear

While a consultation with a potential client is not exactly a job interview with a major corporation where you would wear a dark business suit or similar attire, it is nonetheless a business meeting, and appropriate clothing is called for.

On the other hand, wedding planners are usually creative extroverted people with a flair for fashion and the latest trends. So how do you dress? Somewhere in the middle between dark business clothes and fashion-forward ones would be suitable. You only get one chance to make a first impression and yours should say professional, forward thinking and creative.

Women may wear colored suits, either pant or skirt sets, and separates that are well put together and could include:

- A dress with matching suit jacket (solids are best)

- A skirt (no minis!) and matching suit jacket

- A bright but solid colored pant suit

- A skirt or pants with complementary colored jacket

- Anything black (except jeans)

For creativity, add a funky piece of jewellery, fashionable scarf or dynamite handbag.

For men, the best choice is business casual (no jeans or khakis) which could include:

- Slacks with a matching solid colored sweater

- Suit jacket and pants — no tie

- Slacks and matching knitted turtleneck sweater

- Suit pants or dress slacks with solid color shirt and tie — no jacket

For both men and women: shoes should be absolutely spotless, in good repair (no cracked heels or broken shoe laces) and scuff-free. You will also be expected to dress appropriately so you fit in at any of the wedding events you are to attend. Fitting in does not mean competing with the bridesmaids. Keep it professional and understated (i.e. a suit).

Who Will Attend the Meeting?

In a perfect world your initial client consultation will involve three people: the bride and groom-to-be and you. However, you may be asked to also meet with the mother and father of the bride, the groom's parents or a combination of any of these people as well as the wedding couple. This can be a little more challenging to come to the decision stage as everyone will have their own ideas.

If parents attend, make sure you include the bride in every conversation and speak directly to her (not her mother or fiancé). For instance, if you notice the bride's mother monopolizing the conversation, ask the bride what she thinks. It is important for you to get along well with everyone but it is vital you build a good rapport with the bride.

What to Say

Follow the advice given earlier in this guide for building a relationship. Ask questions about what the clients want, and listen at least twice as much as you talk. Instead of describing all your services, focus specifically on what the clients want, and offer a few ideas for their wedding. Don't worry about someone stealing your ideas and then deciding not to use your services. The fact that you are willing to share a few ideas will leave the impression that you have many more that you haven't shared.

The issue of money, and if your fees and service are worth the cost, is bound to be raised either on the phone or at the meeting. If you followed our script for the telephone call you have already planted the seed in the bride's head that you will take all the stress and worrying out of the planning process and hopefully you won't have to justify your fee during the consultation. If you do get involved in this conversation, remember to focus on the benefits of your services, which include:

- You can find reputable vendors and ensure there are no wedding day "disasters" because you have back-up plans in place.

- You can actually save them money because you can negotiate lower prices with vendors. (This will depend on both your fees and the relationships you have established with vendors. However, you should definitely let them know if – even after paying your fee – the wedding will cost less than if they had organized it themselves.)

- You can save the couple many hours of time. You could show them the checklists of all the details that have to be organized, and ask if they have time to do all those things on top of their busy schedules.

- Remind the couple they can still do any tasks they want to do, but you can take over all the tasks they don't want to do.

- You can come up with lots of options for them, but it is their wedding so they ultimately "call the shots."

- The couple can enjoy a stress-free wedding day.

Remember to focus on what the couple wants. Ask them why they are interested in hiring a wedding planner, and what they think a wedding planner can do for them. They may talk themselves into hiring you!

5.4.3 Your Contract

A wedding planner contract (also known as a "service agreement") should be fairly simple and straightforward so as not to scare away your clients. Design yours to fit the services you decide to offer. You can do this by leaving blanks, which can be filled in later, under the type of service or package. This will also allow you to design a package to suit the needs and desires of the client. Your contract should include:

- Your company name, your name, address and contact information

- The clients name(s), address and contact information

- The date of the wedding (include a space for other events for which service is expected)

- Description of the service(s) being provided

- Maximum number of meetings included in the price

- Cancellation policy

Sample Service Agreement

This agreement is made this _____ day of _____, 20__.

Between: Your Company Name
Your Address
City, State, Zip
(hereinafter referred to as the "Planner")

And: Client(s) Name(s)
Client Address
City, State, Zip
(hereinafter referred to as the "Client")

For: Wedding Planning Services

The Planner agrees to provide the following services to the Client in consideration of the amount specified in the Section titled Fees:

Package (include the name or other designation and a description of the service):

_____

_____

[This next section describes the exact services you are to provide. Include any agreed-upon services that are outside the scope of the above named package.]

Package to also include the services outlined below:

_____

_____

_____

_____

_____

_____

Service, as described above, to be performed on or about the following date(s):

[List specific dates such as these below.]

- *Rehearsal co-ordination:* June 9, 2006
- *Wedding Day co-ordination:* June 10, 2006

Cancellation Policy

In the event the services of the Wedding Planner are no longer required (cancellation of wedding, etc.) the Client agrees to pay a percentage of the total agreed fee, as set out below:

- Forfeiture of deposit if event is cancelled within 30 days of signing of this contract

- XX% of the total fee if event is cancelled within 90 days of signing of this contract

- XX% of the total fee if event is cancelled within 30 days of the scheduled event

Fee Schedule

Package (# or name)	$XXXX
Initial consultation	Free
Subsequent consultations	$XXXX per hour
Vendor visits	$XXXX per visit
Wedding day co-ordination	$XXXX
Rehearsal co-ordination	$XXXX

Total: $XXXX

The client agrees to the total fee as outlined above and to a payment schedule as follows:

Payment Schedule
- 10% deposit upon booking
- 50% of outstanding balance due: /   /
- Remainder of outstanding balance due: /   /

I/We agree to the terms and conditions as set out above:

_____   _____
Client   *Witness*

[Your Company Name] per: _____

- Section for fees to include:
  - List each service to be provided
  - Cost of each service or package to be provided
  - Maximum number of hours worked per day
  - Hourly rate after maximum hours reached
  - Payment terms
  - Deposit schedule
  - Total fee

- Blank section for special considerations (i.e. meal for planner and assistant)

- Signature lines for you and the client(s)

You should have your contract checked by a lawyer before using it. A sample contract is included on pages 246 and 247 to get you started.

5.5 Professional Associations and Certification

As your business grows, you may decide to join a professional association. There are many associations that a wedding planner can join and each offers different benefits.

The Association of Bridal Consultants

The Association of Bridal Consultants ("ABC") is a membership service organization that has been a professional organization for the wedding industry since 1981. ABC's focus is to increase awareness of the wedding business and improve professionalism of members. There are approximately 4,000 ABC members in 26 countries on six continents including wedding consultants, vendors and corporations.

Website: **www.bridalassn.com**

Fees: $165/year (Novice) plus a one-time $35 application fee
$245/year (Consultant)
$175/year (Vendor)
$135/year (Auxilary memberships)
$550/year (Corporate)

Benefits: Regular newsletter, discounts, job placement services, client referrals, information services, professional development programs, feedback on design of brochure, educational seminars and annual conference, business name search, ability to obtain insurance (E&O, liability, health and dental) and certificate reflecting your membership.

Contact: E-mail office@bridalassn.com or phone (860) 355-0464

Association of Certified Professional Wedding Consultants

The Association of Certified Professional Wedding Consultants ("ACPWC") was established in 1990 and is an organization solely for wedding consultants/co-ordinators (i.e. not for vendors or others involved in the wedding industry). Membership is limited to individuals who have taken the ACPWC courses and received a Certificate of Completion.

Website: **www.acpwc.com/members.html**

Fees: $200/year (Active Membership)
$125/year (Affiliate Membership)

Note: Membership is only available upon completing professional development programs and receiving a Certificate of Completion.

Benefits: Monthly membership events, networking opportunities, lead referrals, vendor presentations and continuing education programs.

Contact: E-mail annnola1@earthlink.net or phone (408) 528-9000

Association for Wedding Professionals International

The Association for Wedding Professionals International (AFWPI) is an international organization that was set up to provide a central source of information and referrals for wedding consultants, individuals planning weddings and others who service weddings.

Website: **www.afwpi.com**

Fees:	$102–$285/year (Regular Membership) $150–$425/year (Associate Membership) Fees vary depending on what month you join, plus you pay a one-time setup fee of $25
Benefits:	Referrals, monthly mailing list of brides, discounted services, networking, use of the AWPI logo, listing in the AWPI directory, AWPI website listing, group rates on insurance, quarterly newsletter, seminars, workshop, annual convention, merchant credit card program and assistance in locating suppliers
Contact:	E-mail richard@afwpi.com or phone 800-242-4461

June Wedding, Inc.
An Association for Event Professionals

June Wedding, Inc. An Association for Event Professionals ("JWI") is an internationally renowned and respected membership organization of wedding and event professionals.

Website:	**http://www.junewedding.com/ vendorresources_membership.html**
Fees:	$175/year (Small Business/Sole Proprietor Membership) $275/year (Corporate Membership)
Benefits:	Use of JWI logo and name on business materials, business referrals from JWI and fellow members, quarterly newsletter, company listing at JWI website plus hyperlink to your webpage, membership lists, education programs and discount off JWI workshops and conferences.
Contact:	E-mail robbi@junewedding.com or phone (469) 241-1480

National Black Bridal Association

The National Black Bridal Association (NBBA) is a new association headquartered in Dallas, Texas. The mission of NBBA is to provide a "top-notch" group of professional experts in the wedding industry dedicated to African American weddings.

Website: www.nationalbba.com

Fees: $125/year (General Member)
                  $200/year (Vendor Consultant)

Benefits: Bridal referral service, free web-site advertising/listing, media relations, free photo ad, discounts, listing in the NBBA guide, networking, newsletter and annual conferences.

Contact: E-mail info@nationalbba.com or phone (817) 784-8515

The National Association of Wedding Professionals, Inc.

The National Association of Wedding Professionals, Inc. (NAWP) is an organization of professionals that provide wedding services. The commitment of NAWP is to uphold superior quality and service.

Website: www.nawp.com

Fees: $200/year

Benefits: Share bride industry leads, website advertising, regular meetings, networking opportunities, bridal show, etc.

Contact: E-mail info@nawp.com or phone (941) 728-2592

Weddings Beautiful Worldwide

Weddings Beautiful Worldwide ("WBW") is a division of National Bridal Service ("NBS") for independent wedding consultants. NBS has been in business since 1951 and has a very high standard of excellence. Membership in NBS includes nearly 800 stores and 4,000 wedding consultants throughout the world.

Website: www.weddingsbeautiful.com/membership.htm

Fees: $119 for every six months
                  Note: First six months of membership are free after completing WBW Certification Program

Benefits: Referrals, regional seminars, bi-monthly newsletter, hot-line telephone consultant (to answer your questions about any aspect of wedding business), use of WBW name, trademark and logo, recommended suppliers, national market research reports including facts and information on wedding industry trends, etc.

Contact: E-mail info@weddingsbeautiful.com or phone (804) 288-1220

6. Conclusion

You have reached the end of the *FabJob Guide to Become a Wedding Planner*. Hopefully, this is also the beginning of your new career: helping couples plan a perfect wedding day to enjoy and cherish the memory of forever.

The months and weeks leading up to a wedding are a blur for most couples as they struggle to make key decisions and keep everybody happy. You will remind them to stop and take stock of what is really important—the love that brought them together—and ensure that their day truly reflects that unique love they share.

This guide has covered a lot of ground, including:

- An introduction to wedding planning

- Details about the services you may be asked to provide

- How to help the couple make selections that are right for them

- How to stay organized leading up to and on the big day

- Developing beneficial relationships with vendors in your locale

- Improving your skills to be the best planner you can be

- Finding job openings in the wedding industry

- Starting a wedding planning business

- Selling your services to clients

- And more!

The authors sincerely hope you have enjoyed this guide and will refer back to it frequently as you progress in your career. We wish you fabulous success as a wedding planner, and in all areas of your life.

More Fabulous Books

Find out how to break into the "fab" job of your dreams with FabJob.com career guides. Each 2-in-1 set includes a print book and CD-ROM.

Get Paid to Plan Events

Imagine having an exciting high paying job that lets you use your creativity to organize fun and important events. **FabJob Guide to Become an Event Planner** shows you how to:

- Teach yourself event planning (includes step-by-step advice for planning an event)
- Make your event a success and avoid disasters
- Get a job as an event planner with a corporation, convention center, country club, tourist attraction, resort or other event industry employer
- Start your own event planning business, price your services, and find clients
- Be certified as a professional event planner

Get Paid to Decorate

Imagine having a rewarding high paying job that lets you use your creativity to make homes and businesses beautiful and comfortable. **FabJob Guide to Become an Interior Decorator** shows you how to:

- Teach yourself interior decorating (includes step-by-step decorating instructions)
- Get 10-50% discounts on furniture and materials
- Create an impressive portfolio even if you have no previous paid decorating experience
- Get a job with a retailer, home builder or other interior design industry employer
- Start an interior decorating business, price your services, and find clients

Visit www.FabJob.com to order guides today!

Does Someone You Love Deserve a Fab Job?

Diskette Inside!
Please discharge carefully!!!

Giving a FabJob guide to someone you believe in them and support their dreams. Help them break into the career of their dreams with the ...

- FabJob Guide to **Become a Bed and Breakfast Owner**
- FabJob Guide to **Become a Business Consultant**
- FabJob Guide to **Become a Caterer**
- FabJob Guide to **Become a Celebrity Personal Assistant**
- FabJob Guide to **Become a Children's Book Author**
- FabJob Guide to **Become an Event Planner**
- FabJob Guide to **Become an Etiquette Consultant**
- FabJob Guide to **Become a Fashion Designer**
- FabJob Guide to **Become a Florist**
- FabJob Guide to **Become a Human Resources Specialist**
- FabJob Guide to **Become a Makeup Artist**
- FabJob Guide to **Become a Massage Therapist**
- FabJob Guide to **Become a Model**
- FabJob Guide to **Become a Motivational Speaker**
- FabJob Guide to **Become a Personal Shopper**
- FabJob Guide to **Become a Professional Organizer**
- FabJob Guide to **Become a Public Relations Consultant**
- FabJob Guide to **Become a Super Salesperson**
- **And dozens more fabulous careers!**

Visit FabJob.com for details and special offers